101 Travel Bits:
The Alaska Highway

The Travel Bits™ Series
A division of Tchop Street LLC

Table of Contents

Introduction

Travel Bits™ are not your typical guidebooks. In fact, they aren't guidebooks at all!

Each collection of Travel Bits consists of 101 "bits" of information about one of the great places to visit in the world. This could be a "bit" of history, a "bit" of information on a tourist attraction, or a "bit" of something else interesting about the location.

A Travel Bits collection is not intended to be a guidebook to any particular location. You will not find the maps or pictures you would expect in a guidebook in any Travel Bits collection. No Travel Bits collection contains any pictures. Instead, each book gives you information a typical guidebook ignores: history, fun facts and interesting sights along the way.

This isn't to say that there are no pictures involved in a Travel Bits collection. Each Travel Bits collection is optimized for reading as an e-book. This format makes each Travel Bit interactive, with links to official websites and other information where it is appropriate. Thus, instead of raising the cost of the book to include pictures, we take advantage of the Internet's enormous wealth of information to take you to where the pictures already exist.

In case it isn't obvious, because of the interactive nature of e-books, we highly recommend reading the Travel Bits collections using an e-book reader, as the print versions do not have these interactive features.

We welcome your comments. Please go to the Travel Bits website for information on how to let us know your thoughts.

If you are so inclined, we would love it if you would leave an online review or reviews wherever you purchased this book and let others know how much you enjoyed it.

Please visit our website, www.101travelbits.com, to view other books in the Travel Bits collection and view upcoming titles to add to your collection.

Thank you, and please enjoy this entry in the Travel Bits series!

Travel Bit Number 1: The Alaska Highway

The Alaska Highway is a 1,400 mile road that crosses some of the most inhospitable and least-populated parts of North America. For decades before the Japanese bombed Pearl Harbor in 1941, people had discussed building a road from the Lower 48 states of the United States to America's northernmost territory of Alaska. However, before World War II, no shortage of issues prevented it from happening. Temperatures along the proposed routes to Alaska varied from -80° in winter to 80° in summer. Upon the arrival of summer, the mosquitoes and flies came out for three snow-free months during which they could enjoy a human feast. Any road to Alaska would have to cross mountains, streams and bogs as it traversed a bear-infested forest. Plus, despite some Americans thinking of their neighbor to the north as America Junior, Canada is its own sovereign country that would not take kindly to the appearance of bulldozers and thousands of Americans intending to build a road through their country.

On December 7, 1941, with the bombing of Pearl Harbor, all of the reasons that had prevented a road from being constructed to Alaska quickly disappeared. Suddenly, there were Japanese submarines in the Pacific Ocean that could disrupt the normal means of reaching Alaska by water, and thus, no safe way to supply the territory. To secure access to Alaska, the U.S. Army and a group of civilian contractors built a road that linked the United States and Canada to Alaska within ten months of the bombing of Pearl Harbor. This hastily constructed road gave the United States a guaranteed route to access Alaska throughout the War even if the ocean shipping lines were compromised. Called ALCAN (a contraction of 'Alaska-Canada') during the War, it is now referred to as the Alaska Highway.

After World War II, the U.S. Army turned control of most of the Alaska Highway over to Canada, and the highway built during war became a magnet for tourists looking for an adventure. Today, the Alaska Highway links the town of Dawson Creek, British Columbia with Delta Junction, Alaska, crossing British Columbia, the Yukon and Alaska. For 70 years, the road has been a beacon for tourists looking to complete one of America's greatest road trips.

Travel Bit Number 2: Dawson Creek (Mile 0)

The Alaska Highway begins in the city of Dawson Creek, British Columbia. Dawson Creek sits near the border of British Columbia and Alberta, approximately 360 miles northwest of Edmonton, Alberta.

Despite a similar name, Dawson Creek, British Columbia has no relationship to a similarly named television program popular in the United States during the late 1990s. For years, Dawson Creek was a small farming community on the Canadian frontier. In the 1930s, the railroad arrived in town and was shortly thereafter followed by the U.S. Army, which made Dawson Creek one of its bases during the construction of the Alaska Highway in 1942.

Dawson Creek is named after George Dawson, who surveyed significant portions of Northwestern Canada during the 1880s. Dawson also served the Canadian government as both a chemistry professor and a cartographer. Due to a childhood illness, Dawson stood under five feet tall as an adult, but this disability did not prevent him from making major discoveries as a surveyor; today he is known as one of Canada's greatest scientists.

Today, Dawson Creek remains a farming community, but its economy is also greatly influenced by the oil and gas exploration in the surrounding areas. As the start of the Alaska Highway, nearly 150,000 tourists are also drawn to Dawson Creek yearly, making it their jumping off point for the adventure promised by the long drive to Alaska.

Tourism Dawson Creek:
http://www.tourismdawsoncreek.com/

Travel Bit Number 3: The Two Beginnings of the Alaska Highway (Mile 0)

As the beginning of the Alaska Highway, Dawson Creek provides tourists with not one, but two, places to memorialize their arrival at the beginning of the long road to Alaska. Both are mile markers designated as Mile 0 of the Alaska Highway.

The first — and larger — of these two markers is 'The Gates to the Alaska Highway.' Located next to a busy roundabout at the Northern Alberta Railways Park, the Gates are an arch next to downtown Dawson Creek. Red and blue lettering across the arch welcomes travelers to the first of the 1,400 miles of the Alaska Highway with American and Canadian flags, and a message that "You are now entering the world famous Alaska Highway." It is also believed to be the most photographed place on the entirety of the Alaska Highway.

The second of the markers that memorialize Mile 0 of the Alaska Highway is located in the center of downtown Dawson Creek. It is also the literal center of an intersection, with cars swerving around it at all times of the night and day. Caution for those wanting to take pictures with this marker is recommended, especially for those who would like to see the other end of the Alaska Highway with all bones intact. This semi-dangerous marker is the one that originally denoted the beginning of the Alaska Highway when it opened to tourists in 1948, but thanks to at least one previous accident during which the marker was destroyed, it is no longer the main marker for Mile 0.

Travel Bit Number 4: The 1943 Dawson Creek Fire (Mile 0)

In February 1943, as World War II continued to rage across Europe and the Pacific, the Alaska Highway had been completed and served as a major method for supplying Alaska. At the start of the Alaska Highway, Dawson Creek served as a major staging area for those commencing the long trek up the road. From the frontier town of a few ramshackle buildings Dawson Creek had been prior to the arrival of the U.S. Army, the city had grown into something that would have been unrecognizable as the Dawson Creek of a few years prior, with hundreds of new bunkhouses, warehouses, administration buildings and many other buildings necessary to the construction and operation of a major highway during wartime.

One Dawson Creek building, which was not new but had housed a livery stable prior to the arrival of the Americans, housed all the items that were needed to install a telephone line up the Alaska Highway during the winter of 1943. Unbeknownst to the residents of Dawson Creek, the building also stored a significant amount of dynamite; a separate contractor was using the building to store percussion caps, despite the obvious danger of storing both these items together.

As a nearly entirely newly-built town on the edge of the northern frontier, Dawson Creek lacked a municipal water system. Residents of the town bought drinking water off of a horse-drawn cart by the bucketful, collected rainwater, or melted snow in winter to obtain water. On February 13, 1943, when a fire started in the former livery stable, everyone in town pitched in to try to control the blaze. Without a central water supply, there was little that could be done to suppress the flames.

As the fire burned the former livery stable, a crowd had gathered to both help fight the fire and watch it burn on the winter night. The U.S. soldiers stationed in the town attempted to keep the crowd away, but a fire has a way of drawing attention and they couldn't keep an ever-growing number of people from the area. As the soldiers worked at crowd control, a giant explosion ripped through the building, caused by the dynamite and percussion caps stored in the former stable. The explosion sent everything inside the building flying into the air and it fell in flames across the town and surrounding area.

The explosion completely leveled part of Dawson Creek. Almost no building in town escaped without some damage, be it fire damage, downed walls, or broken windows. Twenty people were killed and over 100 were seriously injured. The town's doctors and nurses were forced to attend to the dead and dying by candlelight, as electricity was entirely cut off in the wake of the disaster. The exact number of those who were injured remains unknown; because of the difficulties facing the doctors and nurses in town, many who were seriously injured did not seek help to keep from taxing the system any more than necessary.

Travel Bit Number 5: How the Alaska Highway Was Built

When the U.S. Army arrived in Canada to build the Alaska Highway in 1942, it found itself in an inhospitable location, tasked not only with building a road but determining where to build that road in a location that had almost no roads of which to speak. Significant portions of the area through which the road would traverse remained almost entirely unexplored; at one point during the construction, what the road builders thought was a small hill turned out to be a 3,000-foot-tall mountain.

To call what the U.S. Army built in 1942 a road, however, is to use the term "road" in its loosest sense. With a goal of completing the highway in nine months, time was the deciding factor in all decisions relating to the building of the initial road to Alaska. As Brigadier General William Hoge, who commanded the building of the Alaska Highway, noted after his time on the road, "We couldn't wait for surveys. Sometimes I'd tell my tree cutters to head off into the bush and shake the tallest tree. Then I'd tell the bulldozer drivers to head for the trembling tree." Problems with building the road were exacerbated by a lack of maps. The only maps General Hoge had were a few he had pulled from old issues of National Geographic.

While today the U.S. Army gets most of the credit for the building of the Alaska Highway, much of that credit actually belongs to civilians who followed the Army. The Public Roads Administration ("PRA") followed the Army; the civilian PRA, consisting mainly of Americans, improved the road in all senses of the word as they moved behind the Army. What little is left of the "original" Alaska Highway is not that which was built by the Army, but that built by the PRA. The men who worked for the PRA came to work on the Alaska Highway voluntarily, despite advertisements that promised work that sounds something less than pleasant. For instance, one read: "Men hired for this job will be required to work and live under the most extreme conditions imaginable. Temperatures will range from 90 degrees above zero to 70 degrees below zero. Men will have to fight swamps, rivers, ice and cold. Mosquitoes, flies and gnats will not only be annoying but will cause bodily harm." Although paid well, the civilian workers who arrived to work on the Alaska Highway often did not last long because, unlike their Army counterparts, they had a choice in the matter of whether they stayed or not. Then again, with advertisements like that, it was somewhat amazing any of the civilian contractors showed up in the first place.

The PRA often found better paths for the Alaska Highway than those mapped out by the U.S. Army. While the U.S. Army had only been interested in getting a road built as fast as possible, the PRA was tasked with building a better road. In almost all places, the surface of the road was improved to make it something that at least resembled what most people considered a road. As it turned out, the Army's idea of a "road" was quite different than the idea of civilians, as they possessed vehicles capable of traversing large trees and small bodies of water which civilians did not.

Thus, from the moment the Alaska Highway was completed, the PRA and other contractors who have followed have always sought to find a better path for the road. The Alaska Highway one now drives is often less a work of the U.S. Army than it is a work of the PRA and contractors who get little to no credit for the significant amount of work they did to give us the road we enjoy today.

Travel Bit Number 6: Rapeseed

If one travels the beginning of the Alaska Highway in late-July or early-August, one agricultural crop stands out in the fields: the yellow flowers of the rapeseed, or canola, plant.

Rapeseed has a long history as a cultivated plant. In India, the oil from rapeseed was used as lamp fuel at least 4,000 years ago; others similarly used it as people spread the plant across the world during the millennia that followed. Upon the invention of the steam engine, rapeseed oil proved a particularly useful lubricant. During World War II, the steam engines on many of the ships used by the navies of the world caused a shortage in rapeseed oil, and Canada stepped in to increase its production. Rapeseed grew well in Canada, even in the short summers of the northern portions of its provinces.

After World War II, the demand for rapeseed oil decreased, and countries with large productions of rapeseed, like Canada, sought other uses for the oil. The rapeseed plants that now proliferate across Canada and the beginning miles of the Alaska Highway arose out of this quest to find a post-war use for rapeseed.

In the early 1970s, scientists at the University of Manitoba bred the modern form of rapeseed to decrease the acid in the oil. The resulting product looked and tasted better than the rapeseed originally cultivated across the world, which had primarily served as a fuel and lubricant. The new plant was given the moniker 'canola' — a combination of 'can' for Canada and 'ola' for oil. The new moniker was created in part to avoid the obvious language issues created by the term 'rapeseed,' and can refer to the plant itself, or the oil that is obtained from the plant's seeds.

Today, in addition to its culinary uses, canola continues to be used as a fuel and lubricant. It is used as a biofuel in many parts of the world, and is the second largest oil crop in the world, after soybeans.

Travel Bit Number 7: Kiskatinaw Bridge (Mile 17)

Just off of the Alaska Highway lies the Kiskatinaw Bridge, the last original bridge on the Alaska Highway. However, calling the Kiskatinaw Bridge either "original" or "on the Alaska Highway" is a stretch. The Kiskatinaw Bridge was built by one of the PRA civilian contractors hired to improve the Alaska Highway after its original construction by the U.S. Army. Thus, the bridge is not the original bridge built by the Army, but the "original" bridge built by the contractors who replaced the Army's hastily constructed bridge.

Likewise, the Kiskatinaw Bridge is not "on the Alaska Highway." Although it is still a functional bridge, like many other places that were at one time located along the Alaska Highway, the road has now been routed around the bridge. While the bridge is still in use, it cannot withstand either the amount of traffic that now travels the Alaska Highway or the large vehicles that now regularly traverse the road.

Today, the Kiskatinaw Bridge is a short drive off of the Alaska Highway. Stretching 561 feet across the Kiskatinaw River, the bridge's timber trusses and surface curve as they cross the river valley, just a few miles from where the Alaska Highway now travels.

Travel Bit Number 8: The Peace River (Mile 34)

A frequently cited statistic along the Alaska Highway is that there are more people who live along the first fifty miles of the Alaska Highway than there are living along the rest of the 1,350 miles of the highway combined. One reason for this disparity in population is the Peace River, which provides water for the agriculture that initially allowed for settlement of this part of the world and continues to provide an economic base for those living along the initial portion of the Alaska Highway.

When initially building the Alaska Highway, the first two cities on the road—Dawson Creek and Fort St. John—were linked by a wilderness road. However, where the road crossed the Peace River, there was no bridge. Instead, during winter, travelers crossed the river via the ice sheet that covered its waters; during summer, a ferry plied the river. Unfortunately for those who wanted to travel between the two cities, for significant parts of the year the Peace River's rushing waters were not traversable, due to high waters or the annual ice breakup.

The U.S. Army could not function without a bridge linking the two communities and set to building a bridge across the Peace River along the old wilderness road. Unfortunately for the U.S. Army, building a permanent structure over the river proved difficult; flooding washed away the first three bridges in quick succession. Finally, a suspension bridge built between 1942 and 1943 survived; it was one of two suspension bridges on the Alaska Highway at that time. However, in 1957, erosion led to the collapse of the suspension bridge, which was rebuilt into the non-suspension bridge that stands today. Today, the only suspension bridge remaining along the Alaska Highway is the bridge crossing the Lower Liard River.

Travel Bit Number 9: Taylor (Mile 35)

Prior to the building of the Peace River Bridge, the ferry that served as the connection across the Peace River was located in Taylor, British Columbia. In 1966, a dam on the Peace River controlled the floods that had wreaked havoc on the towns and bridges along the river until that time.

Today, Taylor is a small community on the shores of the Peace River. Every year, the town hosts the World's Invitational Gold Panning Championships. Gold panning is a simple way to extract gold, in both nugget and flake form, from an area with a gold deposit; its known history begins with the ancient Romans. Today, gold panning is primarily recreational in its use, though it is also used in places where there is a lack of capital for more efficient methods of gold panning or which are too remote for more efficient methods.

Travel Bit Number 10: Natural Gas

Between Dawson Creek and Fort Nelson, much of the small industrial site work along the road is natural gas exploration. In Taylor, there is a $40 million natural gas scrubbing plant and oil refinery. This plant sits at the beginning of a 700-mile-long natural gas pipeline that supplies Vancouver and western Washington with natural gas. Built in 1957, this was the first natural gas pipeline constructed in Canada. Profits from this pipeline have allowed the area to flourish when other locations along the Alaska Highway, which are reliant on boom and bust industries such as timber and metals, have not.

Travel Bit Number 11: The Second Beginning of the Alaska Highway (Mile 47)

One question that arises among travelers on the Alaska Highway is where the Alaska Highway begins and ends. Today, the beginning of the road to Alaska is almost universally considered to be Dawson Creek. On the Alaska end of the road, things are not so clear. In Alaska, there are two potential ends to the road: Delta Junction and Fairbanks.

At the start of World War II, Fairbanks was not far removed from its days as a gold rush town. Founded in 1901 when a businessman's boat ran aground as he attempted to get further upstream, the city was known for much of its history as having the best red light district in the west. Known as the Fairbanks Line, the red light district was founded by an Episcopal Archdeacon and leading city businessman; the semi-legal, much-regulated district flourished until well after the end of World War II.

Although the Alaska Highway is often said to end in Fairbanks—and there is even a marker in downtown announcing the city as such—Delta Junction, 95 miles southeast of Fairbanks, also claims to be the end of the Alaska Highway. The reason is simple: when the U.S. Army arrived to build the Alaska Highway, they never built a road between Fairbanks and Delta Junction, because a road already existed between the two locations. Thus, if you consider the Alaska Highway to be the road the U.S. Army built during World War II, then the highway ends in Delta Junction.

However, this causes a problem for determining the beginning of the Alaska Highway.

If one considers Delta Junction to be the end of the Alaska Highway because there was already a road to Fairbanks when it was constructed, one then has to seriously reconsider whether Dawson Creek is the true beginning of the Alaska Highway. Why? Because a road between Dawson Creek and Fort St. John, the next city on the Alaska Highway, already existed when the Army arrived in Canada to build the Alaska Highway.

Unlike the road between Delta Junction and Fairbanks, however, the road between Dawson Creek and Fort St. John was not much of a road; it more closely resembled an ATV trail or bike path. Moreover, the "road" between Dawson Creek and Fort St. John lacked a bridge over the Peace River. (Travel Bit Number 8.) Thus, when the Army arrived in 1942, while a "road" existed, there still remained the small matters of building a major bridge and creating a wider, more functional road between the two cities. Today, among some travelers on the Alaska Highway, the true beginning of the road remains a topic of argument and debate. For purposes of these Travel Bits, though, we will consider Dawson Creek to be the beginning of the Alaska Highway and Delta Junction to be the end.

Travel Bit Number 12: The Alaska Highway Mileage Issue

Travelers on the Alaska Highway quickly notice that there seems to be some confusion regarding mileage on the highway. Usually, this confusion first arises because someone notices that, although the actual mileage along the road is measured by kilometers and the metric system, the businesses along the road refer to their locations in terms miles and the Imperial system.

The reason for this began during the construction of the Alaska Highway. When the road was built, the difference between kilometers and miles was not a problem. Canada, like the United States, used the Imperial system of distance measurement. Therefore, everything along the road was measured in the only way that made sense to most Americans (and, at the time, Canadians): miles.

In the 1970s, Canada switched from the Imperial system to the metric system. With this change, no small amount of confusion was born for every traveler who ventures to Alaska via the road's winding path through northern Canada.

This confusion arose because, although Canada had switched to the metric system, many of the locations catering to travelers on the Alaska Highway continued to measure their location off of the traditional mile system. This was sometimes out of stubbornness, sometimes out of convenience, and sometimes out of a sense of history. Thus, despite the purported switch to the metric system, locations along the Alaska Highway continued to note their location by using miles, including some places run by the government (like the Mile 80 Rest Area). Put differently, the Watson Lake Signpost Forest — a classic stop along the highway, where people have been leaving signs from their hometowns since the first days of the road's existence — is listed at Mile 635 on the road in guidebooks. (Travel Bit Number 49.)

This alone would be confusing, but the mileage situation gets far worse. From the day it was completed, Canada and the United States have worked to make the Alaska Highway a more efficient drive, mostly through shortening its overall length — as was done with the bypassing of the Kiskatinaw Bridge. (Travel Bit Number 7.) The Alaska Highway has thus gone from its original length of 1,422 miles in 1942 to its current length of 1,390 miles. Thus, while the Signpost Forest is said to be at Mile 635, it is only 613 driving miles from Dawson Creek. Because of this disparity, businesses regularly list both their driving distance from a certain location as well as their historic mileage location on the highway.

Driving the actual road, the confusion only increases. Even though there are kilometer markers and historical mile markers along the road, the historical mile markers are placed at random intervals, seemingly as a purposeful measure to confuse travelers as much as possible. As for the kilometer markers, at multiple locations, the markers manage to skip many kilometers — for example, a mile marker may read KM 615 then the next marker you see reads KM 620, even though you've only traveled two kilometers.

Because that wasn't enough confusion, when Canada switched to the metric system, British Columbia decided it would measure distances along the Alaska Highway in terms of their actual distances from Dawson Creek. However, in the Yukon, the Territorial government decided they would measure distances as conversions of the historical mileage along the highway, ignoring the actual traveled distances. Thus, per the British Columbia government, the British Columbia-Yukon border was located at KM 967.6, while the Yukon government said that the exact same location was at KM 1009. The Yukon has now updated their system to comport with that of British Columbia.

Unfortunately, even this recent change only slightly helps the situation. Even though most locations on the road kept their historic mileage designations, the governments in both British Columbia and the Yukon changed all their official sign posts and mileage signs to the metric system without reference to the former system. And, of course, the metric system doesn't solely apply to the mileage, but to the speed at which you travel. The result of this is that you see advertisements that say things like, "The Stay Inn — Historic Mile 700 — Only 50 km Away" and you still have no idea how far away from this hotel you really are.

Getting to the U.S. only helps this situation marginally, as the United States relies, like the previous Yukon system, on the traditional mileage along the road, ignoring the actual distances in favor of mileage sign posts that indicate your 1942 location along the highway, rather than your modern day location.

Put simply? There is only one accurate milepost on the entire Alaska Highway: Mile Zero in Dawson Creek.

Travel Bit Number 13: Fort St. John (Mile 47)

Today, Fort St. John is the second largest city along the Alaska Highway. It serves as the center of British Columbia's oil and gas industry, though agriculture remains central to the city's economy. It also boasts one of the most unique founding stories for any city in the world.

The original settler of Fort St. John was an escaped slave from Georgia named Daniel Williams. Upon arriving in Fort St. John, Williams took up farming during the short northern British Columbia summers and trapping during its far longer winters. These winter trapping trips could last days or weeks, and when he came home from one long winter hunting trip in 1879, Williams found that he had a new next door neighbor: the Hudson's Bay Company. At the time, the Hudson's Bay Company controlled all of the trading in Northwestern Canada. When Williams arrived to find the Hudson's Bay Company next door, it would be like coming home today from a weekend away to discover someone had built both a new Target and Walmart next door to your home, along with several chain restaurants and a half dozen hotels.

Williams was not happy at the arrival of his new neighbors, and he decided to take care of them in a manner that was not exactly neighborly: he shot at one of the men who had moved into the outpost.

The new neighbor whose welcome to the neighborhood had been heralded with a gun brought charges of attempted murder against Williams, who promptly hired a local character by the name of Banjo Mike to represent him in court. Among the defenses Banjo Mike offered to the jury was that Williams was an excellent shot, and had he wanted to murder the new neighbor, he would have done so in an efficient manner — there would have been no "attempt" at murder. Or, as Banjo Mike put it in court, if Williams had meant to kill the new neighbor, the new neighbor "would not be here today to amuse you with his little story."

The jury hardly deliberated before finding Williams not guilty.

Despite being found not guilty on this original charge and getting a second chance at freedom, Williams would not be deterred from his fight with the Hudson's Bay Company. Upon returning to Fort St. John after being acquitted, Williams proved his ability to go beyond merely *attempting* murder when he *actually* murdered a Mountie over the still-simmering feud with the Hudson's Bay Company (which had not left the less-than-stellar neighborhood, notwithstanding their knowledge of the neighbor who was willing to go to any length to get rid of them).

Unlike the previous shooting, even Banjo Mike couldn't help Williams beat the murder charge the second time around. After being found guilty of murder, Williams found himself at the deadly end of a noose. The Hudson's Bay Company remained in Fort St. John, and the town became the city it is today.

Tourism Fort St. John:
http://tourismfortstjohn.ca/

Travel Bit Number 14: Charlie Lake (Mile 51; Historic Mile 52)

Located about five miles northwest of Fort St. John, Charlie Lake is a natural lake that measures approximately eight miles long and three miles wide. On May 14, 1942, as soldiers were being ferried down the length of Charlie Lake to a construction site along the Alaska Highway, a spring squall unexpectedly blew up on the lake, capsizing the pontoon raft the soldiers had been riding about half a mile from shore.

At the time of the accident, the waters of Charlie Lake still remained frigid from the winter; twelve of the seventeen soldiers aboard the raft drowned in the cold water almost immediately. Five other soldiers clung to the capsized raft; they were only saved because of a local trapper named Gus Hedin. Hedin saw the accident, and immediately set out in his homemade boat—ignoring the storm—to save the five soldiers clinging to the raft. He made three trips to and from the capsized boat to save the soldiers as the storm raged around them.

Today, a memorial to those soldiers who lost their lives sits on the shore of the lake; it was one of the worst accidents to occur during the building of the Alaska Highway.

Travel Bit Number 15: The Explorer Charles E. Bedaux (Mile 51; Historic Mile 52)

In 1934, the residents of Fort St. John became acquainted with the character of Charles E. Bedaux. Bedaux, a self-made millionaire, made his fortune as an industrial management consultant. He had a knack not only for getting extra productivity out of a company's workers, but for shrewd investments. With the money from his work and investments, Bedaux became something of an adventurer and explorer; for example, he traversed the roadless Sahara Desert with a convoy of five cars. In the summer of 1934, Bedaux decided he would conquer the northern Canadian Rocky Mountains.

When Bedaux arrived on the shores of Charlie Lake in the summer of 1934, it was readily apparent that the millionaire was not one to travel without the comforts of home. He arrived in northern Canada with two limousines, five half-tracks (a truck with both wheels and tank-like tracks), several more supply trucks, a float plane, three riverboats, dozens of hired cowboys, and 130 horses. Among his supplies were cases of champagne, caviar, and foie gras; his wife brought along her French maid, while Bedaux brought his valet. There were various other members of the travel party, including a wireless operator, an auto mechanic, two cameramen, a ski wrangler, and a woman whose presence with the group appeared entirely superfluous.

Although some suspected Bedaux of being a German spy—a conspiracy theory that only gained traction when Bedaux later became friends with much of Adolf Hitler's inner circle and became an economic advisor to the Nazis—he apparently only sought an adventure with his trip to Charlie Lake and the Canadian Rockies. Their large traveling party proceeded into the mountains as July came to an end; their traveling speed was hampered both by Mrs. Bedaux's refusal to rise before noon and by the half-tracks, which were entirely unsuited to travel across the rocky peaks. Within a few days of departing Charlie Lake, Bedaux decided to abandon the vehicles. They were promptly driven off cliffs; their drivers abandoned them at the last possible moment as they fell hundreds of feet to the ground below. The two cameramen proved their worth by filming the destruction.

Proceeding thereafter by horseback, the Bedaux party found themselves trapped by snow by the end of September. When spring came and the party was able to return to Fort St. John via the Peace River, they returned a more bedraggled, but still intact, group. While Bedaux made few contributions to the geographical knowledge of the northern Canadian Rockies with this journey, he certainly found the adventure he had been seeking.

As for Bedaux, after this particular adventure, his life took an unexpected turn. As noted, Bedaux became friends with Hitler's inner circle and a Nazi economic advisor. In 1942, American forces captured Bedaux in northern Africa; he was held as a Nazi collaborator. Approximately a year and a half later, Bedaux committed suicide in the Miami safe house where the FBI had housed him.

Travel Bit Number 16: Tourism on the Alaska Highway

In 1946, with World War II over, the United States handed control of the approximately 1,200 miles of the Alaska Highway situated in Canada over to the Canadians. In 1948, the Alaska Highway opened to tourist traffic for the first time.

The Alaska Highway remained mostly dirt and gravel for years; travelers along the road brought extra tires, gas and supplies and still, many cars which started up the road did not ultimately make it to Alaska. Over the years, Canada and the United States have improved the road; the 1980s brought the paving of the last bit of gravel road, and today, except for portions that have washed out or are under construction, it is a fully modern road. Travelers along the road today may encounter car trouble, but it is no longer expected, as it was for much of the highway's history. Having a spare tire and a basic knowledge of your car is still a good idea, but it is no longer a difficult road to drive.

However, that does not make the Alaska Highway a trip for the faint of heart. Gas stations can be over a hundred miles apart on the more remote parts of the road. Anything beyond basic car service is only available in a few places along the 1,400 miles of highway. During winter, the distances between services increase as businesses close for the slow tourist season. During summer, the road regularly washes out in stretches and significant portions of the road at any time are gravel construction zones barely a lane wide. More than a few of the animals commonly found along the road are perfectly able to kill or maim a tourist, and at least some of those are of the two-legged human variety. Car accidents along the Alaska Highway are common; on remote parts of the road, the hulks of crashed semi-trucks and cars remain long after their injured occupants have left, a morbid reminder of the potential of any road for harm.

Travel Bit Number 17: The Cut (Mile 124)

Because speed was the major factor guiding decisions as to the location of the Alaska Highway, the highway as constructed by the U.S. Army in 1942 often bypassed locations where significant work would be required to construct the road. One of the few original exceptions was The Cut, a rock cut travelers arrive at around Mile 124. Here, the Alaska Highway passes through a large and deep cut in the rocks that lie under the northern Canadian soil.

Although there were few rock cuts along the original Alaska Highway — the other major exception being the area around Muncho Lake (Travel Bit Number 34) — those constructing the road dug near the highway obtain gravel for use in construction. These shallow ruts can still be found along the entire length of the original highway.

Today, unlike the original road, the Alaska Highway passes through many deep rock cuts. The PRA began digging these cuts almost immediately after the Army's completion of the original road, and they have been integral in shortening the length of the Alaska Highway.

Travel Bit Number 18: Flooding on the Alaska Highway

From the moment construction began on the Alaska Highway, floods have proven to be a significant and regular problem along the road. In July 1943, the first summer the highway was open, July 9 and 10 brought the most rain people living in the vicinity of the Alaska Highway could remember. Within 200 miles of Fort Nelson (Travel Bit Number 27), twenty-four of the twenty-five bridges on the highway were completely washed away, along with an unknown number of culverts and other small water crossings. The Muskwa River (Travel Bit Number 26) rose 34 feet overnight.

The 1943 rains returned in early-August. Though only four bridges were washed out in the second set of rains, massive mudslides closed portions of the Alaska Highway.

Floods still remain a regular problem along the Alaska Highway. In 2012, there was enough rain to completely wash out the Alaska Highway in several places. Although the road was only out for a few days, there were no supplies reaching some of the isolated towns along the road. On either side of the washouts, travelers were warned not to start up or down the road; not only was there no gas at the towns nearest the washouts, but these towns were in danger of running out of food. With only a few places to stay in each isolated community along the road, there were stranded travelers who found themselves stranded for days, without a place to sleep.

Travel Bit Number 19: Suicide Hill (Mile 145; Historic Mile 148)

As should be clear if you have been reading this book in order, in its earliest days, the Alaska Highway was an unpaved road that was in no way up to modern standards for highways. Even on this sort of road, there were still portions considered worse than others. One of these was the ominously named Suicide Hill.

When originally built, and for several years of its existence, Suicide Hill was the steepest stretch of the Alaska Highway, clocking in at a 32% grade. As a comparison, this made Suicide Hill only slightly flatter than your typical ski jump. Unsurprisingly, it was also one of the more treacherous portions of the highway. This part of the road was so intimidating that those approaching the descent were greeted with a sign reading, "Prepare to Meet Thy Maker."

For at least one person who died on Suicide Hill, the sign was not just a pithy remark but a warning. Cars fared much worse with Suicide Hill; many of them ended their trips up or down the highway at Suicide Hill.

Today, the Alaska Highway passes around Suicide Hill, saving both lives and cars. However, the steep road still cuts down a hill near the highway, the gash it cut through the landscape still there decades after the road bypassed it as a reminder of the hazards previously posed by travel on the Alaska Highway.

Travel Bit Number 20: Sikanni Chief River Bridge (Mile 159)

The first permanent structure on the Alaska Highway was the Sikanni Chief River Bridge. The bridge was completed on October 28, 1942, several weeks before the final completion of the Alaska Highway.

Like much of the Alaska Highway, the Sikanni Chief River Bridge was built by an African-American engineering battalion. In an era where the armed services remained segregated, much of the often unpleasant and unwanted task of building the Alaska Highway — important though it was to the American war effort — fell to African-American battalions. Throughout the building of the Alaska Highway, these soldiers proved more than worthy of the task given them, and are responsible for construction of major portions of the highway.

Building the Sikanni Chief River Bridge was the sort of unpleasant and unwanted task that would cause even modern engineers significant trouble. The location for the bridge was a 300 foot wide portion of the fast-flowing river as it swept through a high-walled gorge. The spruce trees covering the gorge walls made for a beautiful setting, but there was nothing simple about building a bridge in this particular location. The orders for the battalion were simple: complete a permanent bridge that can withstand major flooding in the wilderness, and do it without the benefit of modern technology and finish it as quickly as possible. Today, such a task would take months, and most likely years, from conception to construction.

The battalion completed the bridge in 72 hours.

By the end of World War II, as part of the constant shortening of the road, the Alaska Highway had already been routed around the Sikanni Chief River Bridge built by this African-American battalion. The original bridge stood unused but within view of the new bridge until 1992, a reminder of both the contributions that these battalions made to the construction of the Alaska Highway as well as the segregated nature of the armed forces at that time. In a devastating historical loss, during the summer of 1992 arsonists destroyed the historic bridge, and now only the metal stanchions that once held up the timber frame of the bridge remain.

Travel Bit Number 21: First Nations

The term "First Nations" is used in Canada to designate those aboriginal individuals in Canada who are neither Métis nor Inuit. There are 617 First Nations communities across Canada. First Nations is a general term; a specific First Nations community will usually define itself as a specific Nation or community, and the individuals who belong to that Nation or community usually identify themselves with more specificity. The term 'First Nations' was originally used sometime in the 1970s or early-1980s, and is meant to elevate the First Nations to the status of 'first among equals' with the French and English as the founding nations of modern Canada.

The First Nations communities were truly the first of the three groups to arrive in Canada and lived in Canada for thousands of years before the arrival of the first Europeans. Indeed, in the parts of Canada along the Alaska Highway and elsewhere across Canada, the First Nations communities were vital to the survival of many of the initial Europeans who arrived long after. Along the Alaska Highway, the winter survival techniques of the First Nations were absolutely necessary for survival, and many of those techniques remain vital to life along the Alaska Highway today. As one example, the snowshoes the First Nations communities used to traverse the deep Canadian snows were quickly adopted by the European fur traders and explorers. In their modern form, snowshoes remain in use today, allowing travel across snows that would otherwise be nearly impassable on foot.

Travel Bit Number 22: Trutch Mountain (Mile 176; Historic Mile 191)

Less than two hundred miles down the Alaska Highway, the current length of the road is already fifteen miles shorter than its historic length. One of the major bypasses along the Alaska Highway — and a significant reason for this major shortening of the road — comes at Trutch Mountain.

Until 1987, Trutch Mountain was the second highest point on the Alaska Highway. The portion of the highway near Trutch Mountain was known for its steep, winding path through the forest. Today, after the major re-routing of the Alaska Highway, this section of road is no longer steep, nor winding, nor the second highest point on the Alaska Highway. Most travelers would describe it as unremarkable.

While the old route over Trutch Mountain is no longer part of the Alaska Highway, this former portion of the Alaska Highway is still in use by those involved in gas and oil exploration. This portion of the Alaska Highway lies within the Western Canada Sedimentary Basin, which is one of the richest oil, gas and coal reserves in the world. The first oil well in British Columbia was drilled in the Basin in 1952. Since that time, over 18,000 additional wells have been drilled and the Basin remains the only place in British Columbia to commercially produce oil or gas.

Travel Bit Number 23: Dead Trees

There are many dead trees alongside the Alaska Highway; their deaths are often either the result of forest fires or spruce beetles. Spruce beetles are ¼ inch long beetles which bore through the bark of trees and feed on the layer below the bark. After three to five years, their feeding will have removed a strip of bark from around the entire circumference of the tree in a process known as girdling. Once girdled, the tree will die.

Many of the pine forests along the Alaska Highway are spruce forests; the spruce beetles are always present in spruce forests and will kill trees in small numbers through girdling at any given time. However, during an extremely dry summer, the spruce beetles will become an epidemic and lead to the large-scale destruction of trees along the Alaska Highway. During these periods, as the number of beetles increase, so too do the number of trees they affect. These forests full of dead, dying and felled trees then become forest fire hazards. Once forest fires move through, the forest regenerates and the cycle begins once again.

Travel Bit Number 24: Prophet River Emergency Airstrip (Mile 217)

      Although they are usually not obvious to someone driving the Alaska Highway, at approximately 100 mile intervals there are airstrips near the road. Some of these are still in use, some are for emergency use only, and others have fallen into disrepair. Most of these airstrips predate the Alaska Highway and were built as part of the Northwest Staging Route.

      Prior to the entry of the United States into World War II and the threat of Japanese interruption of shipping in the Pacific, the U.S. and Canada wanted a method to allow communication and some non-sea-based transportation with Alaska. The answer was the Northwest Staging Route, a series of airstrips across northwestern Canada that linked Edmonton, Alberta to Fairbanks, Alaska. Eventually, the airstrip allowed communication and transportation all the way to Russia.

In the early days after the entrance of the United States into World War II, the Northwest Staging Route was a vital means of keeping Alaska connected to the rest of the United States as a Japanese attack on the West Coast remained a constant threat. Although it quickly became known as a safe route for air travel, in its earliest days, it was anything but. On the inaugural flight of thirty-eight planes up the full Northwest Staging Route in January 1942, twenty-seven of the planes were involved in some sort of crash. Despite these initially awful numbers, within a month most of the planes that set off on the first trip had made their eventual way to Fairbanks. Ultimately, twelve planes on that inaugural trip never finished the route. Those are not the the sort of numbers that inspire confidence in air travel.

Today, most of these air strips are abandoned and being reclaimed by nature. The Prophet River Emergency Airstrip is one of the airstrips still available for emergency use and is just a few feet off of the Alaska Highway.

Travel Bit Number 25: CATEL

CATEL—an abbreviation for "Canadian Telephone"— provided a vital part of the Alaska Highway. As part of the construction of the road, the company was charged with completing a $4.3 million project to provide reliable telephone and teletype communication with the outside world for every Army and Air Force installation along the Alaska Highway. With logistical support from the military, CATEL used a civilian work force to do just that. The project was anything but easy. For example, the construction workers discovered the ground was so frozen—even in October—that earth augers were ineffective at drilling holes for the telephone poles. Instead, they had to use dynamite to "drill" holes for the telephone poles.

Until 1963, the system built by CATEL during World War II served the highway, at which point it was replaced by microwave relay stations. The towers housing these newer relay stations that replaced the original system remain a regular sight along the Alaska Highway today; they are spaced at regular intervals along the Canadian portion of the road.

Travel Bit Number 26: Muskwa River (Mile 281)

The lowest point on the Alaska Highway is the bridge over the Muskwa River, just prior to the arrival of the road in Fort Nelson. Within 100 miles of this lowest point on the Alaska Highway, the highway reaches its highest point, at Summit Lake. (Travel Bit Number 31.)

Shortly after leaving Fort Nelson, the Alaska Highway travels through the Muskwa-Kechika Management Area. At almost 16 million acres, the Management Area is approximately the size of Ireland and is the largest wilderness region in the Canadian Rockies. The purpose of the Muskwa-Kechika Management Area, as stated in the act that established it, is to "maintain in perpetuity the wilderness quality, and the diversity and abundance of wildlife and the ecosystems on which it depends, while allowing resource development and use in parts of the Muskwa-Kechika Management Area designated for those purposes, including recreation, hunting, trapping, timber harvesting, mineral exploration and mining, and oil and gas exploration and development."

Because it has the largest abundance and diversity of large, wild mammals in North America, some refer to it as the Serengeti of the North. Drivers on the Alaska Highway are almost guaranteed to see large mammals on the section of the drive through the Muskwa-Kechika Management Area, and likely of more than one species.

Muskwa-Kechika Management Area:
http://www.muskwa-kechika.com/

Travel Bit Number 27: Fort Nelson (Mile 283; Historic Mile 300)

Fort Nelson, like most of the other towns in northwestern Canada with names using the term "fort," was originally established as an outpost of the Hudson's Bay Company. These forts were not military establishments, but fortified locations where trappers and others living in the area could come to sell furs or buy supplies. The current city of Fort Nelson is not at the original site established by the Hudson's Bay Company; the city is on its fifth site along the Fort Nelson and Muskwa Rivers. The location of the original Fort Nelson is of some dispute, but there is no dispute as to its end: it burned to the ground in 1812.

Today, Fort Nelson is the last city along the Alaska Highway to have rail service connecting it to the rest of Canada and the United States. Beyond Fort Nelson, communities can only be reached by car or plane.

Prior to the construction of the Alaska Highway, Fort Nelson was also the home of a trader named Tommy Clark, who served as the Hudson's Bay Company manager for the Fort Nelson post. At some point in his life, Clark had lost one of his eyes. He had replaced this lost eye with a glass one. Or, more accurately, which he had replaced it with many glass eyes, which he changed out to suit the occasion. For example, on Sundays, he sported a glass eye that included a cross, and he had another eye featuring a Union Jack. He even had one brown eye to match the non-glass eye. More than one traveler who made it to Fort Nelson during Clark's service as the manager of the post commented on his choice of "eye wear" in the reports and journals they sent home and kept as part of their own adventures in the north.

Travel Bit Number 28: The World's Largest Chopstick Factory (Mile 283; Historic Mile 300)

For several years, Fort Nelson—a Canadian city on the edge of the wilderness with fewer than 4,000 residents—had the distinction of being home to the world's largest chopstick factory.

Yes, the world's largest chopstick factory.

The forest that surrounds Fort Nelson is composed of aspen, which is the preferred wood for making the ubiquitous, disposable wooden chopsticks associated with Asian food throughout not just North America, but Asia as well.

At its height, the factory made eight million chopsticks a day destined for the Japanese chopstick market. Unfortunately, the only way the factory was economically viable was through government subsidies. As soon as the Canadian government stopped subsidizing the factory, it closed shop; today, Japan gets its chopsticks from Russia and China.

Travel Bit Number 29: Dall and Stone Sheep vs. Bighorn Sheep

Some don't consider the Alaska Highway to be a true wilderness until it leaves Fort Nelson. Although there is a great deal of wildlife to be seen prior to Fort Nelson, the amount that exists along the way increases dramatically almost immediately after you leave Fort Nelson.

One of the more common animals seen along this portion of the Alaska Highway is the Stone Sheep—a close relative of the better known Dall Sheep. Dall Sheep, which are prevalent in the Yukon and Alaska, are a pure white wild sheep; the Stone Sheep more commonly seen in British Columbia are extremely similar to Dall Sheep, but instead of a pure white coat have at least some gray and black color in their wool. The two sheep are so closely related that the Stone Sheep is considered a subspecies of the Dall Sheep, and some research now suggests they are the same species with different color variations. Together, the two types of sheep are known as the "Thinhorn Sheep" because of the size and shape of their horns. Stone Sheep frequent areas around the Alaska Highway, particularly the portion of the road near Muncho Lake. (Travel Bit Number 34.)

The Dall and Stone Sheep are closely related to the Bighorn Sheep that inhabit the Rocky Mountains in the Lower 48. Bighorn Sheep are larger than their Canadian and Alaskan counterparts, and their horns are large and curled close to their heads. Dall and Stone Sheep have thinner and longer horns than Bighorn Sheep. The sheep one sees along the Alaska Highway are always either Dall or Stone Sheep; there are no Bighorn Sheep in this portion of the Rockies.

Travel Bit Number 30: Canadian Rocky Mountains

Like the increase in the wilderness and number of animals after Fort Nelson, the scenery just after leaving Fort Nelson also makes a dramatic change. While there are mountains before getting to Fort Nelson, the road after Fort Nelson climbs into the Canadian Rocky Mountains. Instead of rounded mountains and mountain-like foothills, these are the stereotypical rocky crags one thinks of when thinking of mountains. For approximately 200 miles after Fort Nelson, the Alaska Highway travels through some of the most scenic vistas of its entire route.

The beautiful stretch of road past Fort Nelson was one of the last sections of the Alaska Highway to be routed when the original path of the road was determined. Some portions of this part of the highway were not even routed until well into the summer of 1942, long after actual construction of most of the Alaska Highway had begun.

Less than fifty miles from Fort Nelson, Steamboat Mountain rises 3,000 feet above the valleys that surround it. Unlike some of its rockier neighbors, Steamboat Mountain doesn't look as if it would be difficult to get around; its slopes don't appear steep when viewed from a distance. When the engineers plotting the route of the Alaska Highway approached Steamboat Mountain, however, they could not find a pass over its seemingly friendly slopes. Only a chance encounter with a local trapper allowed the engineers to find the pass over the mountain.

Although the engineers plotting the route for the Alaska Highway could build a road over Steamboat Mountain, a path through the mountains at a lower level was preferable. After showing them the high pass, the trapper took one of the engineers down to the valley to show him how to cross the mountains at the preferred lower elevation.

During this trip to the valley, the men camped at the confluence of two major rivers in the area — the Muskwa and the Tetsa — which gently flowed past their scenic campsite. As a storm blew up overnight, the formerly tame rivers began to rise. While dawn approached, the rising rivers suddenly began to roar. The two men scrambled out of their tents and on to higher ground just as a wall of water, rocks, and trees swept over what had been their campsite. The flood ended almost as quickly as it had begun, but when the two men returned to their campsite, nothing of their possessions or campsite remained. After this bit of excitement, the trapper unceremoniously abandoned the engineer, who was forced to find his own way back to Fort Nelson. One suspects the engineer didn't have the most pleasant words to say about his abandonment.

Travel Bit Number 31: Summit Lake (Mile 374; Historic Mile 392)

The highest point on the Alaska Highway is Summit Lake, in the Canadian Rocky Mountains. The pass over the mountains at Summit Lake is not particularly high in terms of mountain passes; it crosses the mountains at approximately 4,250 feet above sea level.

Despite the relatively low elevation of the pass at Summit Lake, it is still high enough that one can run into snow or sleet even in the middle of the summer as one crosses the pass. Summit Lake itself regularly has ice on its surface well into June, and the hiking paths into the mountains surrounding the pass can be snow-covered throughout the summer.

Travel Bit Number 32: Hoodoos (Mile 376)

After beginning the descent from Summit Lake, a somewhat unique geographic feature characterizes several areas near the Alaska Highway that are accessible to those willing to take a short detour or hike. This unique geographic feature is the hoodoo.

A hoodoo is typically a pillar of soft rock, topped with a boulder formed of harder rock. As the softer rock erodes, the harder rock at the top of the pillar protects the soft rock below from eroding as quickly as the softer rock around it. The resulting pillar rises from the ground below, a thin column of rock, often with a large rock that appears precariously balanced on the top. Usually, hoodoos are found in deserts. The best known and largest concentration of hoodoos in the world are found in Bryce Canyon National Park in Utah.

Although this part of British Columbia is not a desert, it is still one of the few locations in the world where one can see hoodoos. Although there are some near the Alaska Highway that are accessible to anyone willing to hike for a few minutes, reaching the largest concentration of the hoodoos requires one to get off of the road for a true wilderness hike of several days.

Travel Bit Number 33: The Number of Travelers on the Alaska Highway

As the Alaska Highway reaches the true wilderness of northern British Columbia and becomes a remote road, the lack of people driving the road becomes obvious. Even at the height of summer, one can drive for long periods of time without seeing another car.

Approximately 300,000 people travel the Alaska Highway each year. Most people traveling the Alaska Highway only use a portion of the road, rather than driving it all the way from Dawson Creek to Delta Junction and points beyond. Overall, fewer than 90,000 people annually arrive in Alaska via the Alaska Highway.

To put those numbers in perspective, the busiest stretches of highway in the Lower 48 handle over 300,000 cars per day. On the Alaska Highway, fewer than fifteen cars on average pass over any stretch of the remote portions of the Alaska Highway in any given hour. The Alaska Highway is, even at its busiest, a sparsely traveled road.

Travel Bit Number 34: Muncho Lake (Mile 436; Historic Mile 456)

One of the most unexpected sights along the Alaska Highway is Muncho Lake. Although it is a large lake—the word "Muncho" means "Big Lake" in the local Tagish language—its size is not the most striking feature of the lake; its most striking feature is its color. Even though it is almost 2,700 feet above sea level, Muncho Lake is the aqua color of the Caribbean, a strange and seemingly out-of-place color in an area where snow is a possibility during any month of the year. On clear days when there is little to no wind, the surrounding mountains reflect in the lake's surface, creating one of the world's greatest photo opportunities.

The Caribbean color of Muncho Lake is the result of copper oxide that leaks from the surrounding bedrock into the water. While it now makes for a gorgeous drive, when the highway was built during World War II, this portion of the road was one of the most difficult and expensive to build because its construction required significant excavation of the cliffs surrounding the lake. By the time it was completed, more than 100 tons of explosives had been used to construct the road around Muncho Lake. One unexpected construction cost consisted of the replacement cost for excavation equipment, as it was fairly common for the construction vehicles to tumble from the cliffs around the lake into the deep waters below.

Today, the Alaska Highway takes a stunning path along the lake's eastern shore. It meanders around the shoreline for several miles, sometimes a mere strip of land with cliffs on one side and the lake on the other, with little room between the road and either hazard. While there are no real towns along Muncho Lake, because of the recreation opportunities in the area, this is one of the more developed areas in the 319 miles between Fort Nelson and Watson Lake.

Travel Bit Number 35: Mineral Lick (Mile 454)

Shortly after the Alaska Highway leaves the shores of Muncho Lake on its way to Alaska, the road passes a natural mineral lick. Natural mineral licks are found around the world, and typically provide animals in the region a method to obtain minerals vital to their good health. For example, one mineral commonly found in licks is calcium, which aids the animals gathering at the lick in bone development and strength.

The mineral licks lining the road in this area attract large animals — particularly Stone Sheep. A short hike off of the road leads to the steep banks of the Trout River. Like the area along the road, the banks of the Trout River are mineral-rich. From a viewpoint at the top of the ridge, one can regularly see many of the large herbivores living in this part of the world visiting these mineral-rich banks, such as caribou, elk and Stone Sheep.

Travel Bit Number 36: The Telegraph Line to Europe

During the 1850s, Western Union wanted to lay a telegraph wire between the United States and Europe. After several failed attempts to lay a Trans-Atlantic line, in 1865, crews of men arrived on both sides of the Bering Strait and in Canada to do what they had failed to do in the Atlantic: lay a telegraph line to Europe. However, instead of crossing the Atlantic, this telegraph line would cross the short length across the Bering Strait and traverse the long length of Russia.

At the time of the construction of the telegraph line, Russia included what is today Alaska; it would not be sold to the United States until 1867. (Travel Bit Number 94.) The project became known variously as the Russian-American Telegraph, Western Union Telegraph Expedition or Collins Overland Telegraph.

The crews of men sent to Russia and Canada worked diligently to lay the telegraph line across a vast area of wilderness. However, in July 1866, Western Union crews succeeded in laying a trans-Atlantic telegraph cable. However, the crews in Canada and Russia didn't hear about the success for a year, and continued to work until 1867.

After $3 million and a significant amount of work, the planned telegraph line across the Bering Strait was stopped. The crews abandoned the telegraph where it stood, leaving both telegraph poles and the valuable materials for the line itself in the woods. For years afterward, First Nations communities used what they could salvage from the abandoned lines and camps for their own use and as trade goods.

While the telegraph line did not ultimately succeed in getting to Russia and Europe, the crews who worked on the project were ultimately able to put the information they learned while laying the line to good use: when the United States began to consider purchasing Alaska from the Russians, they looked to the crew members to provide information on the potential value of the resources that could be found in the vast wilderness of Alaska.

Travel Bit Number 37: Lower Liard River Bridge (Mile 477)

There are hundreds of water crossings along the Alaska Highway. From unnoticed culverts crossing unnamed streams that only carry water during rainstorms to some of the biggest rivers in the world, water is a near-constant presence near the road. These streams and rivers provide many opportunities to those who wish to fish, canoe or otherwise enjoy their natural beauty.

The water courses along the Alaska Highway also provide an opportunity to see many types of bridges. However, the crossing at the Lower Liard River is the only suspension bridge on the Alaska Highway, after a second suspension bridge at the Peace River crossing between Dawson Creek and Fort St. John was destroyed in 1957. (Travel Bit Number 8.)

Travel Bit Number 38: The Deadly Moose

The assumption of many visitors traveling the Alaska Highway is that the most dangerous animal they will encounter is the bear. However, this assumption is wrong.

The most dangerous animal along the Alaska Highway is the moose.

Moose attack more people every year than bears and wolves combined. The only wild animal that attacks more humans across the world is the hippopotamus. While injuries inflicted by moose are generally not severe, this does not mean that they cannot seriously injure or kill a person. In 1995, a moose on the University of Alaska at Anchorage campus stomped a man to death. An Alaskan wildlife biologist has been widely quoted as saying that "the best practice around moose is to go away around a moose. Assume every moose is a serial killer standing in the middle of the trail with a loaded gun."

Moose also constantly pose a danger to drivers. The average moose stands five to six and a half feet tall at the shoulder; like their smaller and more common deer relatives, many deadly car accidents every year are the result of moose-car collisions. One study estimated that one in a thousand Alaskan commuters would be involved in a moose-car collision in any given year. There aren't any studies on moose-car collisions on the Alaska Highway, but one only needs to see a single moose-car accident to realize that it is not a collision the car is likely to win.

Travel Bit Number 39: Liard River Hot Springs (Mile 478; Historic Mile 496)

Of all the stops along the Alaska Highway, few are more popular with travelers than the Liard River Hot Springs. A series of natural hot springs that are now part of a Provincial Park, Liard River Hot Springs are a chance for weary travelers to get off of the road and soak in warm, natural pools that remain open all year long.

The first known record of the Liard River Hot Springs comes from 1898, when explorers arrived in the area and noted the presence of the springs. In the mid-1920s, a pilot doing reconnaissance for mineral exploration stopped at the springs to inquire about a trapper and his daughter living in the area. Upon his return to civilization, his stories of the hot springs inspired incredible stories stating — falsely — that the area was home to not only monkeys and parrots, but even dinosaurs. The hot springs were nicknamed the Liard Tropical Valley, and remained a part of Canada subject to fantastic, and usually untrue, stories for years afterward. As it turned out, the rumors about the presence of the hot springs were true, even if the details of the creatures one would find there were not accurate.

During World War II, the soldiers working on the portion of the road near the hot springs used them as a natural bath; they were also the first to build paths and boardwalks to the hot springs. As soon as the road opened to tourist travel in 1948, it became one of the biggest draws along the highway. Today, tens of thousands of visitors stop for a warm soak every year.

While not palm trees, the plants in the hot springs and surrounding pools are typically found in warmer parts of Canada lying hundreds of miles to the south; there are even fourteen different species of orchids around the springs. Across the world, hot springs are often described as islands that are isolated pockets of climate within a larger climate; an ecosystem within an ecosystem. Liard River Hot Springs is no exception.

A study of the vegetation around the Liard River Hot Springs found 82 species of plants growing near the springs, of which 43 were temperate species not normally found in the area. For many of these 43 plants, the hot springs were the furthest north they had ever been discovered. There are multiple species of carnivorous plants that call the hot springs home, in addition to orchids and ferns that are not normally found anywhere near this part of the world.

When it comes to animal life, the hot springs attract a large number of animals thanks to their warmth and open water throughout the year. On the smaller side, tiny lake chub call the hot springs home; these small fish dart beneath the feet of visitors walking the boardwalks across the warm swamps to the hot springs and are uniquely able to withstand the warm water and chemical content of the hot springs.

On the larger side, the hot springs are also home to many moose, who placidly graze along the boardwalks, happy for an easy meal in these Canadian tropics. There is some evidence of a snail that exists only in the vicinity of the hot springs, but a lack of study means no one knows for sure if the snail exists. Years ago, pranksters let a snapping turtle loose in the swamps around the pools, despite it being well north of its normal habitat. Thanks to the warm water of the pools, though, the snapping turtle survived for years, evading capture by the park rangers and providing a unique wildlife viewing experience for this part of Canada.

Travel Bit Number 40: Fort Halkett and Smith River Falls (Mile 496)

From 1829 to 1875, Fort Halkett was a Hudson's Bay Company trading post on the Liard River. As previously noted, such forts were not forts in the typical military sense. Although they provided protection to the individuals living within their walls, these forts existed mainly to trade with those living in the area. In this part of Canada, that trading consisted primarily of fur trading with the First Nations people and the few other trappers living in the vicinity.

Today, the former location of Fort Halkett is within Fort Halkett Provincial Park. Fort Halkett Provincial Park is also the location of Smith River Falls, a pretty waterfall a short drive and hike off of the Alaska Highway. While pretty in the summer, Smith River Falls has the dubious winter distinction of being the location of the fourth coldest temperature ever recorded in North America.

Travel Bit Number 41: Million Dollar Valley (Mile 495; Historic Mile 514)

Despite traversing a wilderness area in an era where air travel was less than fifty years old, the Northwest Staging Route was known to be extremely safe, despite initial issues. (Travel Bit Number 24.) However, its reputation for safety didn't mean there weren't problems along the route. In its early days, there were no published maps for pilots to use for navigation along the Northwest Staging Route; any maps that existed were hand drawn—often on the spot—for those who were unfamiliar with the route.

This was not the most reliable method of navigation.

In January 1942, three B-26 Marauder pilots discovered exactly how poor a method of navigation this could be. These three pilots and their crews had been handed some of the aforementioned hand drawn maps and sent on their way to the next air strip with a simple message: "You can't miss it!"

They missed it.

In a snow shower, the pilots were unable to find the next air strip and ran out of fuel. They crash landed their planes in a valley near the local river. Unfortunately, this being northern Canada, the local river was not really near anything useful to people who had just crash landed, such as a road or a town. After a local pilot found the crash landed planes, it took a week to evacuate all the pilots and crewmembers. However, the planes had to be abandoned in the valley.

The Valley where the planes had landed — a previously unnamed and unremarkable valley — was given the moniker "The Million Dollar Valley." The reason was simple: it was the supposed value of the abandoned planes in the valley.

After World War II, only a few of the B-26 Marauders of the type that crashed into the Million Dollar Valley survived; the vast majority were scrapped for the value of their metal. Over three months in 1971, an aircraft enthusiast sent a team in to rescue the abandoned planes in the hopes of restoring a very rare aircraft. He was successful; all three planes are now either restored or in the process of being restored into airworthy planes.

Travel Bit Number 42: Grizzly Bears vs. Black Bears

If one species of animal is associated with the Alaska Highway more than any other, it is the bear. There are two species one sees along the Alaska Highway: the black bear and the grizzly bear. There are thousands of each in the woods surrounding the road, and for the most part, they exist peacefully with the many humans who travel along the road each year.

Grizzly bears (also known as brown bears) are generally larger than their black bear cousins. The two bears can be differentiated otherwise by going through a series of three characteristics: hump, facial profile and ears. Grizzly bears have a large hump on their shoulders which black bears lack. The profile of a grizzly bear's face is relatively flat; its forehead goes straight to its nose, while a black bear has a distinct break between its forehead and nose. As for ears, a grizzly bear's are short and round, in contrast to the tall ears of the black bear.

While grizzly bears are typically known as being more aggressive than black bears, there are some who believe that the black bears along the Alaska Highway are a particularly aggressive group. A black bear at Liard River Hot Springs (Travel Bit Number 39) killed two visitors to the park; the trails at the park and one of the two hot spring pools are regularly closed because of aggressive black bears who reside in the area. Just a few years ago, a black bear attacked a couple at their home near Delta Junction, the end of the Alaska Highway. The husband was killed in between his home and the lake on whose shores the couple resided. Thus, while identification of the bears in the area is useful, one should give all the bears who live in the area a wide berth, as both types are capable of injuring or killing those who do not.

Travel Bit Number 43: Allen's Lookout (Mile 551; Historic Mile 570)

High above the Liard River, a group of bluffs provide a beautiful view of the river and the surrounding landscape to current travelers on the Alaska Highway. However, today's pleasant view once provided a more sinister view for previous visitors to the area.

Allen's Lookout, now a picnic and rest area along the highway, once provided a lookout to bandits. These bandits used the extensive view provided by the high vantage point of Allen's Lookout to scout boats plying the waters of the Liard River. Upon finding a promising boat, the bandits could easily make their way to the shores of the river and rob the unsuspecting boats bringing valuable furs and gold in and out of northern Canada.

Travel Bit Number 44: The American Bison

Perhaps the large mammal that travelers along the Alaska Highway are most likely to see is an animal that they may not expect: the American Bison. Apparently finding the grasses that grow along the Alaska Highway irresistible, bison are almost constantly present along at least one stretch of the highway.

All of the bison along the Alaska Highway are Wood Bison. Wood Bison are a distinct subspecies from the Plains Bison that one sees at Yellowstone or elsewhere in the American West. Although the two subspecies appear very similar, among other differences, the Wood Bison are significantly larger than their southern cousins. Unlike many Plains Bison you see in the Lower 48, the Wood Bison along the Alaska Highway are free range. Their "wild" cousins in the Lower 48 are, in reality, contained within various parks and large preserves and are not truly free range.

While most now refer to these large animals as bison, rather than buffalo, calling these animals "bison" ignores at least one significant fact: across North America, most bison you see (with a very few exceptions, such as those at Yellowstone) are not entirely bison. Almost all bison alive today have some cattle blood in them. When bison nearly went extinct in the 1800s, those that were left were bred with captive cattle; their descendants now roam as wild bison, despite their partially domesticated ancestry. The amount of cattle DNA left in these wild bison is now less than two percent, but it remains as a reminder of how close America's largest land mammal came to extinction. Today, there are over 7,000 Wood Bison ranging across Canada and Alaska — a far cry from the days when the only thing that saved this subspecies from extinction was the discovery of an unknown herd of 200 animals in Alberta in 1957, and from which all Wood Bison today descend.

Travel Bit Number 45: BC-Yukon Border (Mile 558)

The Alaska Highway first crosses the border between British Columbia and the Yukon at Mile 558, but because the highway runs along the border for many miles, one passes between the province and the territory several times before officially entering the Yukon.

In an era where there are satellite images of every part of the globe and seemingly nowhere remains unexplored, there are few things about the surface of the earth that remain a mystery. However, along the Alaska Highway, a geographic question remains unanswered: how many times does the Alaska Highway crosses the border between British Columbia and the Yukon?

There is no dispute that the Alaska Highway crosses the border between British Columbia and the Yukon several times over the course of approximately 180 miles. However, expert sources put the number of crossings at anywhere from six to nine, a quirk that is a result of the near-constant routing and re-routing of the Alaska Highway. At some point over the course of these crossings, the highway returns from the Yukon back into British Columbia for over forty miles, eventually reaching the official crossing from British Columbia into the Yukon at Mile 605 and Historic Mile 627, just outside Watson Lake.

Travel Bit Number 46: Contact Creek (Mile 568; Historic Mile 588)

One reason the U.S. Army was able to complete the construction of the Alaska Highway as quickly as it did was by constructing the highway in multiple sections at the same time. Four main construction groups set out to construct the highway. The southern half of the construction went from Dawson Creek to Whitehorse, with separate groups starting at Dawson Creek and Whitehorse, each working toward each other. The northern half of the construction crew worked from Whitehorse to Delta Junction, again with separate groups starting at Whitehorse and Delta Junction and working toward each other.

The southern portion of the Alaska Highway was the first portion of the road to be completed. On September 24, 1942, a bulldozer headed north from Dawson Creek met a bulldozer headed south from Whitehorse, and one half of the Alaska Highway was completed. The creek where the two bulldozers met was christened Contact Creek in honor of the occasion, and within a week, daily supply runs between Dawson Creek and Whitehorse had commenced.

Travel Bit Number 47: Slim Williams

Prior to World War II and the construction of the Alaska Highway, many people advocated for the building of a road linking Alaska to the Canadian highway system and, via those highways, to the Lower 48 states of the United States. Slim Williams, an Alaskan gold prospector, did not intend to be one of those advocates, but thanks to an accidental comment, he became the most colorful, and likely the most famous, advocate for a road.

In 1932, life on the Alaskan frontier remained extremely hard; men and women eked out an existence by trading furs or prospecting for gold. The Great Depression had entered its third and worst year, though in Chicago, a bit of levity arrived with the Century of Progress Fair. Held on the shores of Lake Michigan, the Fair gave almost forty million visitors the chance to see new cars, gadgets of the future and even the first baseball All-Star game as an antidote to the struggles of everyday life.

In Alaska, 3,500 miles from the Century of Progress Fair, Slim Williams found himself at a local trading post, procuring supplies and talking with his neighbors about the Fair. One of the men he spoke with noted the intention of one of Slim's rival prospectors to travel to Chicago via dog sled to attend. Upon hearing this, Slim mentioned in passing that he, too, intended to travel to Chicago via dog sled to attend the Fair.

Slim initially had no intention of following through on this bit of hyperbole.

However, two weeks later, making another run to the trading post for supplies, Slim unexpectedly saw his name in the newspaper. It seemed that Slim's prideful boast two weeks earlier constituted news in an area where moose outnumbered people, and the newspaper now announced his intention to travel to Chicago via dog sled.

Not only that, this particular bit of uplifting news had done the 1930s version of going viral: it was already or would soon be printed in newspapers in all forty-eight of the states.

Not one to back out of a commitment — even one he had not intended to make — Slim began preparations to drive his sled dogs from Alaska to Chicago. He had planned to make the trip without outside backing, but while making preparations, another advocate for a road from the Lower 48 to Alaska approached Slim. This other, well-off advocate for building a road offered Slim $300 if he would just add a slight detour to Washington, D.C. as part of his trip. In Washington, Slim would then lobby for a road to Alaska. Slim accepted the offer and found himself with an extra 700 miles tacked on to his trip to Chicago.

In November 1932, Slim Williams and his dog team set out for the Lower 48. Along the way, Slim nearly drowned, a wolf killed one of his sled dogs, and by May — still in Canada — a decided lack of snow meant dog sledding became quite a bit more difficult. Wheels for the dog sled were procured, and ten months after he had set out, Slim arrived at the Fair in September 1933. For six weeks, Slim became one of the most popular exhibits at the Fair, eating and sleeping with his dogs on the shores of Lake Michigan, before heading on to Washington.

Upon the completion of the last part of the journey, Slim arrived in Washington an extremely popular man; he hadn't even changed out of his dog sledding clothes before he was meeting with none other than the President, Franklin D. Roosevelt. Apparently, the $300 spent to get Slim to Washington to meet with influential people had been money well-spent.

Unfortunately, despite meeting with people in high places, the Great Depression meant that there was little support—or, more importantly, financial backing—for a road to Alaska. It would take nearly another decade, and the danger of war, before the road for which Slim advocated came to fruition.

As for Slim, in 1939, he repeated the trek, this time traveling from Alaska to Seattle. On this second trip, despite the lack of a road, he made the trip via motorcycle. With the opening of the Alaska Highway shortly after his second trip, Slim became a popular lecturer and regaled audiences across the United States with his tales from Alaska. Slim passed away in the mid-1970s at the age of 93.

Travel Bit Number 48: Watson Lake (Mile 613; Historic Mile 635)

Watson Lake, with a population of under 1,500 people, is the third biggest city in the Yukon. Although the city shares its name with a local lake, the lake travelers on the Alaska Highway see as they pass through the city is Wye Lake, an entirely different lake than the one for which the city is named.

The lake and city of Watson Lake take their names from Francis "Frank" Watson, an American-born man who originally came to the Yukon at the age of 14 with his father to prospect for gold as part of the Klondike gold rush. When Watson's father went back to the United States in 1900, Watson remained in the Yukon. In 1903, Watson settled on the shores of what would become known as Watson Lake, though at the time it had the rather unoriginal name of Fish Lake.

Watson married Adela Stone, a member of the Kaska Dena First Nation. Today, the descendants of their marriage still remain in the area, which also remains the traditional home to the Liard River First Nation of the Kaska Dena. The Kaska Dena were traditionally nomadic, and traveled in small family groups across a large part of northwestern Canada using dog teams and packs. Their traditional territory includes over ten percent of British Columbia in addition to parts of the Yukon; for much of its length, the Alaska Highway travels through this traditional territory.

Travel Bit Number 49: Signpost Forest (Mile 613; Historic Mile 635)

On the outskirts of Watson Lake lies one of the most famous sights along the Alaska Highway: the Signpost Forest.

The origins of the Signpost Forest, like so much along the Alaska Highway, have their roots in World War II. Carl Lindley, a soldier working on repairing signs along the highway during the War, had the unfortunate luck to have a dump truck run over his foot while on the job. While recuperating and probably dreaming of home, he decided he would create a sign pointing the way to his hometown and post it along the road near Watson Lake. Lindley's original sign consisted of an arrow pointing southeast, and informed Lindley's fellow soldiers they were a mere 2,835 miles from Danville, Illinois.

Not happy to let Danville get all the notoriety, others soldiers followed Lindley's lead and put up signs detailing the general direction and mileage to their own hometowns. Once tourists started heading up the Alaska Highway, they continued the tradition and eventually expanded it to include town signs with populations, elevations and general statements about the relative merit of wherever they might be from to the collection of signposts in Watson Lake.

Today, there are thousands of signs nailed to posts and trees on the outskirts of Watson Lake in the Signpost Forest. Every year, the town erects new poles in the Forest, and people use them to post ever more signs, dragged thousands of miles from the Lower 48 and places further afield for the sole reason of leaving a mark that a person stopped 635 miles or so up the Alaska Highway. One estimate is that there are 2,500 to 4,000 new signs added each year; there are now over 75,000 signs descended from the original one Carl Lindley erected 75 years ago. Sadly, the original sign and post are lost to history, but in 1992, Carl Lindley helped erect a replica sign to celebrate the Signpost Forest's fiftieth birthday.

Travel Bit Number 50: Our Lady of the Yukon Church (Mile 620; Historic Mile 642)

In September 1861, decades before the Klondike gold rush, Father Zépharin Gascon, a Catholic priest and missionary, arrived in the Yukon. Father Gascon was only the first of many missionaries who would ultimately find themselves in the Yukon, attempting to convert hearts to their respective faiths or keep those who might stray without their guidance upon the religious path.

Father Gascon's foray into the Yukon was not only temporary, it was fruitless. He failed to convert the local postmaster with whom he wintered from 1861-1962, the only erson he apparently attempted to convert during his brief sojourn in the Yukon. While Father Gascon appreciated the hospitality of his Protestant host, the postmaster remained wedded to his non-Catholic roots.

With the Klondike gold rush, additional missionaries arrived, seeking converts among both the First Nations people and the prospectors alike. Like many of those who arrived around this time, the priests and missionaries came to the territory with little to no experience in the ways of the back country. They had to learn to live in a manner entirely foreign to them, with dog sleds as transportation and the building of churches their personal responsibility, from the cutting of the trees to the placement of the steeple. Unlike Father Gascon, however, these priests remained in the Yukon to build a community of the faithful.

While the Yukon remained isolated in the decades that followed the Klondike gold rush, with the arrival of the Alaska Highway, the mission churches, like so much else in this part of the world, only grew in number and importance. Along the route of the Alaska Highway, numerous small churches were built to serve both the locals and the travelers who ventured up the early highway. Our Lady of the Yukon Church is one of these early mission churches. It was built in 1956 along the highway, and remains alongside the road's path today.

Travel Bit Number 51: Albert Creek Bird Observatory (Mile 621)

The Yukon is a prime location for bird watchers. As winter slowly warms into spring, hundreds of species of birds return to their summer homes from locations further south, where they spend the inhospitable winter months. Taking advantage of this profusion of bird life, the Albert Creek Bird Observatory operates a seasonal bird banding operation from late-April until early-June in a location just outside Watson Lake. Over the course of just a few spring weeks, the Albert Creek Bird Observatory will not only see hundreds of birds from dozens of species, but will band over 1,000 birds.

Some of the birds banded at the Albert Creek Bird Observatory will have arrived there after long, annual migrations. For example, the Blue-Winged Teal—one of the most vocal duck species—is an occasional visitor to the Observatory. Blue-Winged Teals are one of the last birds to arrive back in the Yukon after spending their winters as far south as Brazil and Peru. Wilson's Warbler is one of the most common species seen at the Observatory after its return to the Yukon from its Mexican and Central American winter. The very small bird is one of the easiest for novice bird watchers to spot; both the male and female are bright yellow, and it generally has little fear of humans.

Travel Bit Number 52: Fireweed

Perhaps the most ubiquitous plant along the Alaska Highway is fireweed. Although there are probably more numerous species of plants, fireweed, with is gaudy pink/purple flowers, demands to be noticed far more than most of the plants growing along the road. That it grows in forest clearings, such as those made by the road and forest fires, only makes it more noticeable.

Fireweed is a pioneer species — a species that is among the first to colonize a disrupted or damaged ecosystem. When Mt. St. Helens erupted in 1980, fireweed was one of the first plant species to grow on the devastated slopes of the mountain. While it is prevalent along the Alaska Highway, fireweed occurs across much of the United States and all of the Canadian provinces. It is also the national flower of Russia, and was one of the first flowers to bloom after the World War II bombing of London.

Travel Bit Number 53: Rancheria River (Mile 677)

Although the Klondike gold rush is the most famous of the gold rushes in the Yukon (Travel Bit Number 59), smaller gold rushes were a regular occurrence before and after the Klondike gold rush. A prospector would find a small bit of gold in a stream, word of the find would get out, and a minor gold rush would be on. The Rancheria River was the site of one of these small gold rushes around 1875. Over the course of three seasons, approximately 2,000 men found their way to this small area of the Yukon, in search of their fortune. The gold rush ultimately produced about $2 million in gold before the prospectors moved on to newer strikes and the never-ending promise of quick riches found in the various gold fields that sprang up in northern Canada and Alaska. At Rancheria, the prospectors left little behind but the name of the river, which is an unusual Spanish word found in a part of the world where English and First Nations names are the rule.

Today, one might find some gold flakes in the rivers and streams where this minor gold rush once occurred. However, today's main prospectors in the area are large, multinational companies who purchase the mineral rights to large swaths of land instead of short stretches of river. Instead of gold, today the prospectors look for zinc and silver.

Travel Bit Number 54: Continental Divide (Mile 698; Historic Mile 722)

At Historic Mile 722, the Alaska Highway crosses the Continental Divide of the Americas, also known as the Great Divide. On one side of this Divide, water flows into the Yukon River watershed. From the Yukon River watershed, it flows into the Bering Sea and Pacific Ocean, 2,300 miles away. On the other side of the Divide, water flows into the Mackenzie River watershed before emptying into the Beaufort Sea, which is part of the Arctic Ocean, over 2,650 miles away — and even further from its ultimate destination in the Atlantic Ocean.

The Continental Divide of the Americas is the most famous of the drainage divides in the world; it travels from Seward, Alaska to the tip of South America. On one side of the Divide, water ultimately flows into the Atlantic Ocean; on the other side, the Pacific Ocean. For most of its length, it roughly follows two mountain chains: the Andes Mountains in South America, and the Rocky Mountains in North America.

In the Yukon and on to Alaska, long before anyone would have known the reason behind it, life on the western side of the Divide was generally far easier than life on the eastern side. The western side remained far more populated than the eastern side for nearly as long as humans had lived in the region. The reason behind this was simple: on the western side, salmon from the Pacific Ocean could migrate up the Yukon River watershed and provide a reliable food source for the population. On the eastern side of the Divide, no such food source could be found as the watershed did not drain to an area with salmon. Although people lived on the eastern side, because there was no regular food source, they became nomadic out of necessity and the region never became as populous as the western side.

Travel Bit Number 55: Forest Fires

Those traveling the Alaska Highway in late summer as the land dries out are likely to see smoke from forest fires somewhere along the route. The results of these forest fires are visible at many locations along the road, with large swaths of burned areas in various states of regrowth.

The size of the fires that burn across this part of the world are enormous. For example, almost every summer, Alaskans are subject to over 500 wildfires. The fires usually burn over 1.7 million acres, which is the equivalent of burning the entire state of Delaware to the ground every year. In bad years, it is even worse. For example, in 2004, during July and August, over 6.5 million acres burned; the total acreage burned was an area the size of Maryland.

Thankfully, this portion of the world is sparsely populated, so the fires rarely threaten people. Usually, the only people threatened by the fires are the firefighters who arrive to keep them under control, and the dangers they face are often not directly related to the fires they have arrived to fight. A bear recently attacked a firefighter as he walked outside of his Alaskan firefighting camp; other firefighters die from heart attacks while doing their jobs. The brave men and women who fight these fires are also subject to some unexpected dangers; in 1979, a firefighter died of drowning. Apparently, he was swimming near the fire camp when the accident that led to his death occurred. Oddly enough, he is not the only firefighter in this region who has drowned; three other firefighters have died in the exact same and unexpected manner in northern Canada and Alaska.

Travel Bit Number 56: Teslin Lake (Mile 776)

Two bridges claim to be the longest water spans on the Alaska Highway: the Peace River Bridge (Travel Bit Number 8) and the Nisutlin Bay Bridge, crossing the Nisutlin River as it becomes part of Teslin Lake. As of the publication date of this edition, the actual longest bridge has yet to be identified, though it seems one could easily solve the dispute with nothing more than a tape measurer. If anyone can solve this dispute for us, whether by tape measurer or other means, please drop us a line using the contact page of our website.

Teslin Lake is approximately seventy-five miles long and up to three miles wide and spans the border between the Yukon and British Columbia. The lake is popular with sport fishermen for an abundance of Lake Trout, but it is also home to ten other species of sport fish, including Chinook and Chum Salmon. On one of the longest journeys of any salmon swimming upstream, those salmon which are caught in Teslin Lake have already swum over two thousand miles from the outlet of the Yukon River in the Bering Sea by the time they arrive in Teslin Lake.

During the Klondike gold rush, Teslin Lake was part of the Canadian overland route to the gold fields. Steam-powered boats plied the waters of Teslin Lake as they made their way toward the northern part of the Yukon. Until the arrival of the Alaska Highway, Teslin Lake was part of the main route to Whitehorse, Dawson City and the interior of the Yukon, providing a much slower but reliable way to reach one of the remotest portions of North America.

Travel Bit Number 57: The Teslin Taxi (Mile 777; Historic Mile 804)

The area around Teslin Lake is home to the Tlingit, one of the largest First Nations communities. Perhaps the most famous member of the community was George Johnston, the son of a Tlingit chief. For approximately twenty years beginning in 1910, Johnston photographed his fellow Tlingit community members as they went about their daily lives. Although he only had a small brownie camera and a rough dark room in his cabin, Johnston documented the lives of those around him as they existed in a world where fur trapping and hunting were the only methods of survival. Johnston's hobby has become an invaluable sociological contribution to the modern world.

However, it is the Teslin Taxi that was Johnston's more colorful contribution to history.

In 1928, Johnston found himself with an excess amount of cash after a lucrative fur trapping season. And so, Johnston bought himself a 1928 Chevrolet and had it shipped by paddlewheel boat to his home at Teslin Lake, where he planned to operate a taxi service.

It would be a rather limited taxi service, as there were only four miles of crude road in the area.

Fortunately for Johnston, his fellow fur trappers and First Nations members mostly needed his services over the long Yukon winter. Johnston would take the car up and down the ice of Teslin Lake, dropping off people as needed to hunt and trap at a charge of two dollars a ride. Although it was still a limited taxi service, it saved people many miles of walking or dog sledding during the coldest part of the year.

When the Alaska Highway arrived in 1942, the four miles of road near Teslin Lake became part of the much longer road, and Johnston's taxi services were no longer needed. However, his taxi still sits in the museum in Teslin that bears his name, a tribute to ingenuity and life before the highway brought more than a handful of miles of roads to the area.

Travel Bit Number 58: Dog Sledding

  Before the arrival of the Alaska Highway and before snowmobiles allowed quick travel across the winter landscape of northern Canada and Alaska, the residents relied on their dogs and dog sleds for transportation. While not as fast as the snowmobiles that have largely replaced them, dog sleds were a relatively quick mode of transportation across the frozen rivers, lakes and landscapes of this part of the country and allowed people to live in places that would otherwise have been entirely cut off during the winter months.

  During the Klondike gold rush, dogs were one of the most valued commodities for prospectors and those attempting to get to the gold fields. At the height of the gold rush, a single dog would cost anywhere from $250-$400 — approximately $7,000-$12,000 today; there were reports that some dogs were fetching $1,000, or over $30,000 in today's dollars. With at least six dogs necessary to pull a sled, gathering a team of dogs was a costly project.

Until the 1960s, dog sleds remained a major method of transportation in northern Canada and Alaska; they were still delivering mail during the winter in some locations. Today, some still use dog sleds for transportation, but they are now mainly used for racing, such as for the Iditarod or the Yukon Quest (Travel Bit Number 68). In Alaska, the city of Tok is known as the Sled Dog Capital of Alaska (Travel Bit Number 98); a sled dog trail runs along twenty miles of the Alaska Highway outside the city. Tok is also home to the Race of Champions, the largest dog sled sprint race in Alaska and one-third of the Triple Crown of dog sledding (the other two races in the Triple Crown of dog sledding being the Fur Rendezvous in Anchorage and the North American Championship in Fairbanks).

The dogs now used for racing are almost all mixed breed dogs, sometimes referred to as "Alaskan Huskies." Typically, sled dogs weigh from 45-60 pounds, though they will vary from as little as 35 to over 70 pounds. A typical musher will attempt to match both the sizes of the dogs in a team as well as their gaits, both for longer races as well as the short, sprint races.

Travel Bit Number 59: The History of the Klondike Gold Rush

In 1896, along a tributary of the Klondike River, four prospectors — three men (George Washington Carmack (an American prospector), Skookum Jim Mason (also known as Keish), and Dawson Charlie (also known as Káa Goox)) and a woman (Kate Carmack (also known as Shaaw Tláa, the Tagish wife of Carmack, brother of Mason and aunt of Charlie) — acted on a tip from another local prospector and came across huge quantities of gold. Either George Carmack or Skookum Jim actually discovered the gold, Carmack was credited with the discovery because of worries by the group that the authorities wouldn't recognize the claim of Skookum Jim, who was First Nations.

Within two weeks of the discovery of gold, every potential claim along the water route that would become known as Bonanza Creek had been claimed. Due to the remoteness of the Yukon, it took months before word of the gold strike leaked out to the world beyond the north woods, but once it did, the Klondike gold rush was on.

In the five years of the Klondike gold rush, over 100,000 people had set out for the Yukon despite the harsh reality of the life they would face there. These included men who were already famous, as well as those whose time in the Yukon would make them famous. The former group included Wyatt Earp; he arrived in Dawson City to play the card game faro after fleeing the murder indictment that resulted from the gunfight at the OK Corral. The latter included Jack London, who made his fortune off of the stories he told of his time in the Yukon. (Travel Bit Number 74.) The gold rush burned out quickly; in 1899, gold had been found in Nome, Alaska, and many who had found themselves in the Yukon or had originally set out for the Yukon headed to Nome and the potential fortunes to be found there.

Less than half of those who struck out for the Yukon ever made it to the gold fields they sought. Many abandoned the quest before reaching the Yukon; the population of Vancouver doubled during the Klondike gold rush and that of Edmonton tripled. Of those who reached the Yukon, only 15,000 to 20,000 men and women ever reached the point where they actually prospected for gold. A minute portion of those people found the fortunes they sought, though over $1 billion of gold at today's values was eventually pulled from the creeks and ground at or near Bonanza Creek. Ultimately, there was likely more money to be found in selling goods and services to the prospectors, both in the Yukon and on the way to the Yukon. One of those men, Fred Trump, grandfather of President Donald Trump, earned his initial fortune running the Arctic Restaurant and Hotel in Lake Bennett, along one of the trails to the gold fields.

At its peak, the total population of the Yukon was 27,219 people. Dawson City, at the heart of the gold rush, briefly became the largest city north of San Francisco. After that, the population began a steady decline as people gave up prospecting or headed elsewhere to seek new gold claims. Other than during World War II, when the influx of soldiers and workers artificially and temporarily increased the population of the territory, it took until 1991 for the population of the Yukon to return to the level it had reached during the gold rush era.

Travel Bit Number 60: McClintock Bay (Mile 861)

From late-March until early-May, one can see an amazing natural sight just a few feet from the Alaska Highway: over 10,000 waterfowl—mostly Trumpeter and Tundra Swans—arrive each year on the waters at McClintock Bay on Marsh Lake. For a few weeks each year, the Bay provides some of the only open water in the area for those birds who are migrating back north from their southern winter homes. Just as importantly, the water of the Bay is shallow, rich in food and provides high visibility of any predators in the area, making it an ideal stop for birds who may have flown thousands of miles with few or no breaks in their migration to arrive there.

The Pacific Flyway, of which McClintock Bay is a part, is home to the annual migration of 63,000 Tundra Swans. At any given time when the Bay is the only open water in a sea of otherwise iced-in lakes and streams, over 1,000 Tundra Swans will be at the lake, resting in waves before moving further north.

The rarer Trumpeter Swans—whose worldwide population is only 46,000—are the real draw of McClintock Bay. At any given time during the spring migration, a full 10% of the world's population of Trumpeter Swans will be on the Bay. Trumpeter Swans came close to extinction; at the turn of the 20th century, there were no known Trumpeter Swans left in the world. Thankfully, in 1933, approximately seventy Trumpeter Swans were discovered, all of whom lived near remote hot springs in Yellowstone National Park. Two decades later, a larger population of Trumpeter Swans was found in Alaska, but from these two groups, the entirety of the world's Trumpeter Swan population has descended, and the birds are no longer threatened as a species.

Travel Bit Number 61: Yukon River (Mile 867; Historic Mile 897)

As the Alaska Highway crosses the Lewes Bridge at Historic Mile 897 of the Alaska Highway, travelers on the road get their first glimpse of the Yukon River, the main river in both the Yukon and Alaska. At nearly 2,000 miles from its start here at the edge of Marsh Lake to where it ends in the Bering Sea, the Yukon is the third, fourth or fifth longest river in North America, depending on who is doing the measuring. This depends on who is doing the measuring. Quite likely, these are the same people who are in charge of counting the border crossings between the Yukon and British Columbia. (Travel Bit Number 45.)

Despite its length and importance to the Yukon and Alaska, there are only four vehicle bridges along the entire length of the Yukon River. Even at Dawson City, the second biggest city in the Yukon, former capital of the territory, and site of the Klondike gold rush, the only way to cross the river with your vehicle is via ferry.

The flow of the Yukon River is mostly south to north; its headwaters flow from near the Pacific Ocean in northern British Columbia to the Bering Sea (the exact headwaters of the Yukon River are disputed, with two lakes in northern British Columbia being the leading contenders for the title). This orientation was vital to the Yukon during the Klondike Gold Rush, because it meant fortune seekers were able to cross the mountains at the Pacific Ocean and then float downstream on the Yukon River and its headwaters to the gold fields in the northern Yukon.

Today, the Yukon River's waters are mostly traveled by canoeists and kayakers. The Yukon River Quest is the longest annual canoe/kayak race in the world and travels the waters of the River between Whitehorse and Dawson City. Although now famous for its recreational uses, the Yukon River remains a dangerous body of water even in summer. In addition to flowing deceptively quickly, the temperature of the river never rises much above freezing. A canoeist or kayaker who falls into the water only has a few seconds before the cold begins to incapacitate him or her; hypothermia is a real danger any time of the year, including the middle of summer.

Travel Bit Number 62: White Pass & Yukon Railroad (Mile 879)

Thanks to the Yukon River's south to north orientation and its headwaters' proximity to the Pacific Ocean, it became the most popular route to the Klondike gold fields. Unfortunately for those hoping to strike it rich, to get to the Yukon River, they still had to cross the mountains that stood between its headwaters and the Pacific Ocean. Although the distance between the Pacific and the Yukon River headwaters wasn't great, the mountain passes through them still proved a formidable obstacle to would-be prospectors.

One of these passes, the White Pass, connected Skagway, Alaska with the interior. The nearby Chilkoot Trail connected Dyea, Alaska with the interior. The White Pass had one distinct advantage over the Chilkoot Trail: it was nearly 500 feet lower in elevation, and thus a presumably easier pass to cross, despite being slightly longer. Reality proved different, however, as the White Pass was plagued with mud and difficult conditions that gave it the nickname "Dead Horse Trail"; in one summer alone, over 3,000 horses and pack animals perished as the prospectors pushed north.

In 1898, capitalizing on the Klondike gold rush, three companies were created to build a railroad over the White Pass and into the interior. The three companies were necessitated by the construction of the railroad in two different countries, with the governments of one state and two provinces involved.

Only two months after construction began, the first engine began service on the first four completed miles of the railroad, becoming the northernmost railroad in the northern hemisphere at that time. A year later, the railroad had crossed the 3,000 foot pass and reached Lake Bennett, where prospectors could embark for the gold fields via the Yukon River route. By 1900, almost two years to the day after the opening of the first four miles, the railroad reached Whitehorse, allowing prospectors to bypass the two major sets of rapids on the Yukon River and providing a relatively short trip from Whitehorse to Dawson City and the gold fields.

The White Pass and Yukon Railroad proved invaluable to the builders of the Alaska Highway, who were able to transport building materials from the port at Skagway to the northern headquarters of the Alaska Highway in Whitehorse. However, in 1982, after over 80 years in operation, a downturn in the Yukon economy forced the closing of the railroad. Today, the White Pass and Yukon Railroad has reopened approximately sixty miles of the original line to Whitehorse for tourist use; approximately 300,000 passengers now take the train over the course of an average summer season.

As for the original trail over the Chilkoot Pass that the White Pass & Yukon Railroad bypassed with its completion in 1900, today it is part of the Klondike Gold Rush International Historical Park. Hikers can make their way over the same pass that the prospectors headed for the Klondike Gold Rush once used, trekking thirty-three miles over the pass from the Pacific Ocean to the headwaters of the Yukon River.

Travel Bit Number 63: McCrae (Mile 880; Historic Mile 910)

For nearly a year during World War II, one of the busiest places along the Alaska Highway—if not the busiest part of the highway—was a Quonset hut outside of Whitehorse. This Quonset hut, in a place called McCrae, was home to one of the few distractions available for the soldiers working on the road: a movie theater.

McCrae began life as a flag stop on the White Pass & Yukon Railroad in 1900. During World War II, McCrae became the site of not just a theater, but a full military camp, with warehouses, maintenance shops and everything needed to support soldiers building a road through the wilderness.

At only a few miles outside of Whitehorse, the military camp at McCrae provided a respite for not just soldiers building the highway, but locals from Whitehorse. In addition to the movie theater, the camp hosted dances and had a store and recreation center. And, in 1943, McCrae hosted the first live national radio broadcast from northern Canada. As part of the North American premiere of the Irving Berlin movie, "This Is the Army," the Americans threw a party carried live over the telephone line that had been built alongside the Alaska Highway by CATEL. (Travel Bit Number 25.) To help celebrate the broadcast, one of the stars of the musical arrived on the Alaska Highway, long before his second career as a politician took off: Ronald Reagan.

Travel Bit Number 64: Miles Canyon (Mile 882)

Along the water route from the headwaters of the Yukon to the gold fields at Dawson City, there were only two major hazards: the White Horse Rapids, which gave the city that grew up around them its name, and Miles Canyon, just upriver from the White Horse Rapids.

Known as the Grand Canyon of the Yukon for both its size and beauty, the walls of Miles Canyon rose vertically from one of the two main sets of rapids on the Yukon River to provide a natural hazard to anyone wanting to navigate the river. Prospectors who reached Miles Canyon faced a difficult choice. They could either hire a pilot to take their boats and supplies through the Canyon, or they could wait for a tram built across a log road around the rapids. In either case, with thousands of prospectors heading to the Klondike, a bottleneck formed at the entrance to the Canyon. The small city that developed at the bottleneck came to be known as Canyon City.

By 1900, with the gold rush mostly over and the White Pass & Yukon Railroad completed (Travel Bit Number 62), the boom ended and the rush of prospectors to the Klondike dried up. After three summers in existence, Canyon City closed up shop and its residents moved to Whitehorse, just north of the Canyon.

Today, over a century later, one can still see holes at the top of Miles Canyon where the tramway bed was excavated, including depressions in the tramway route where the long-rotted ties were leveled and supported the log rails.

Travel Bit Number 65: Whitehorse (Mile 887; Historic Mile 918)

Whitehorse, the biggest city on the Alaska Highway, is halfway between its beginning and end. Before a hydroelectric damming project in 1958, the location where Whitehorse now sits was home to one of the two large sets of rapids on the Yukon River, which were said to look like the mane of a white horse; like Miles Canyon, the rapids led to a bottleneck of prospectors and a city grew up where the bottleneck stranded them. When the White Pass & Yukon Railroad arrived in 1900 on the downstream side of the rapids, the city became a permanently habited location.

For the decades between the Klondike gold rush and World War II, Whitehorse had the good fortune to sit at the terminus of the White Pass & Yukon railroad. People and freight wishing to head to the Yukon capital of Dawson City and the rest of the interior Yukon would start their overland or water journeys in Whitehorse. The city, while small, thus catered to travelers and those working and living in the interior of northern Canada.

The city likely would have remained a small city, but for the decision of the builders of the Alaska Highway to make it the headquarters of the northern sector of the road, and the most important supply location along the route — a situation made possible by the White Pass & Yukon railroad's location in the city. Suddenly, a sleepy frontier town became, almost literally overnight, a bustling epicenter of construction for thousands of soldiers and civilian workers. With the completion of the Alaska Highway, Dawson City, which had been the city built by the Klondike gold rush and the capital of the territory, suddenly found itself with second tier status, as it was not reachable by car, truck or railroad. In 1952, the territory moved the capital from Dawson City to Whitehorse, where it remains today.

Today, Whitehorse is a jumping off point for adventurers to northern Canada. Canoeists, hikers, hunters, dog mushers and those looking for wilderness excursions of every sort begin their journeys in Whitehorse, which is known as the least polluted city in the world. In Whitehorse, travelers headed either way on the Alaska Highway have a chance to resupply and eat a fast food meal for the first time in hundreds of miles. Its airport, which first opened in 1920, serves numerous cities in Canada, and during the summer has weekly flight service to Europe. Oddly enough, despite this European service, there is no regular service from Whitehorse to anywhere in the United States, including Alaska — which is less than fifty air miles away.

Travel Bit Number 66: The Whitehorse Liquor Store (Mile 887; Historic Mile 918)

Before the construction of the Alaska Highway, Whitehorse was an unincorporated town that remained relatively isolated. However, when the Americans made the small town their headquarters for the construction of the Alaska Highway, its isolation ended. Almost overnight, Whitehorse went from a town of 400 people to one home to 20,000 people.

Within Whitehorse, one place quickly became more popular than anywhere else: the town's lone liquor store. Despite high prices — whiskey and rum cost $35 a quart, or over $525 per quart in today's dollars — pictures from World War II show lines of men snaking down the street as they waited for a chance to buy any liquor that was available. At one point, the liquor store got two box cars full of beer, only to be sold out by the end of the day. The store had to adopt a policy of opening when a shipment arrived, and closing as soon as they ran out of it, often only opening for two or three hours at a time.

Travel Bit Number 67: S.S. Klondike (Mile 887; Historic Mile 918)

Sternwheelers — large, shallow-hulled boats with a steam-powered wheel at their back which gave rise to their name — were one of the main modes of transportation in the Yukon for much of the early 1900s. Although not unique to the Yukon, the sternwheeler found the most use in this northern outpost of civilization, where it was uniquely suited to the shallow, but otherwise navigable, Yukon River and its tributaries. Over the course of ninety years beginning in 1866, over 250 sternwheelers plied the waters of the Yukon and its tributaries.

Although they navigated many waterways in the Yukon, the original main route of the sternwheelers took them from Lake Bennett — where the two main passes from the Pacific converged after crossing the mountains guarding the coast — to Canyon City. At Canyon City, passengers had to disembark, as the sternwheelers could not navigate either the rapids at Miles Canyon (Travel Bit Number 64) or those at Whitehorse (Travel Bit Number 65). After bypassing the two sets of rapids, travelers boarded a different sternwheeler in Whitehorse for the easy downstream journey to the gold fields at Dawson City. When the White Pass & Yukon railroad was completed in 1899, travelers were able to make the journey from the Pacific to the gold fields with only a brief stop in Whitehorse, where they transferred from rail to the sternwheelers.

The river distance between Whitehorse and Dawson City was approximately 460 miles. On the upstream trip from Dawson City to Whitehorse, the trip took approximately four to five days; the boat made five to seven stops along the trip for wood with which the steam to run the boat was created. The trip downstream took half the time, as the boats traveled twice as quickly. Though a faster trip, the downstream portion may have been more dangerous; remaining in the channel with the strong current was a difficult task for even the experienced captains. The short summers in the Yukon meant that the sternwheelers were only operable for four to five months each year before ice forced the boats into winter berths.

Most of the 250 sternwheelers that once traveled the Yukon waters have long since disappeared, but a few remain. One of these is the S.S. Klondike, which sits in a park in downtown Whitehorse and is open to the public as a Canadian National Historic Site. The S.S. Klondike holds a place in history as the last sternwheeler that operated on the Yukon River. Built in 1929 by a subsidiary of the White Pass & Yukon Railroad, the original S.S. Klondike operated for seven years before sinking. The sternwheeler sitting in downtown Whitehorse is technically the Klondike II, an exact replica of the ship that came before it. The S.S. Klondike ended regular service in 1952, but for three years after ending regular service, it became a passenger ship providing tourists and travelers with an experience that had been commonplace only a few years earlier. However, in 1955, even this service stopped, and the S.S. Klondike took its place in history as the last sternwheeler working in the Yukon.

Travel Bit Number 68: The Yukon Quest (Mile 887; Historic Mile 918)

Every February, Whitehorse is home to what is considered by many to be the most difficult annual dog sled race in the world: the Yukon Quest. Running from downtown Whitehorse to Fairbanks, Alaska in odd-numbered years and Fairbanks to Whitehorse in even-numbered years, the Yukon Quest is a 1,000 mile long test of survival skills and endurance. The race course crosses four mountains and temperatures along the route regularly reach -60 degrees Fahrenheit, even without considering wind chill. The race takes ten to sixteen days to complete, based on weather, trail conditions and obstacles encountered along the way.

Participants in the race are expected to be entirely self-sufficient in a tribute to those who settled northern Canada and Alaska and were entirely reliant on their dogs and dog sleds to survive the long winters. As part of this tribute, there are limited checkpoints and few mandated rest periods for race participants, unlike in the Iditarod. The self-reliance aspect of the race truly extends to every aspect of the race. Mushers and their dog teams regularly encounter wildlife along the route. In the early 1990s, a moose attached the dogs of one musher. The musher promptly killed the moose with an axe before it could kill his dogs and strand him in the deep Canadian wilderness. However, per the rules of the race, before he could continue on, the musher had to butcher the moose and carry it out with him. The Yukon Quest is not a race for the faint of heart. Or those lacking the ability to butcher one of the largest land mammals in the world in sub-zero temperatures while somewhere in the middle of the north woods wilderness.

Official Yukon Quest Website:
    http://www.yukonquest.com/

Travel Bit Number 69: The Cremation of Sam McGee

There are strange things done in the midnight sun
  By the men who moil for gold;
The Arctic trails have their secret tales
  That would make your blood run cold;
The northern lights have seen queer sights,
  But the queerest they ever did see
Was that night on the marge of Lake Lebarge
  I cremated Sam McGee.

So begins and ends The Cremation of Sam McGee, a poem published by Robert Service in 1907. The poem concerns the cremation of a prospector who froze to death in the Yukon, as told by his friend who had been tasked with performing the dead man's cremation. It is quite likely the most popular poem ever written about the Yukon or the gold rush era and has been popular since the day it was first published.

The popularity of the poem proved particularly troubling for one man: the real Sam McGee. When writing his poem, Robert Service saw the name 'Sam McGee' on a receipt that came to him as part of his job as a bank teller; it rhymed with the word 'Tennessee' and therefore would fit well into a poem he was working on. Sam McGee gave permission for the poet to use his name, despite being very much alive and un-cremated. In his very real and alive life, Sam McGee worked as a road builder who prospected on the side. He built the Canyon Creek Bridge, which still stands along the Alaska Highway. (Travel Bit Number 76.)

McGee had no idea the poem would prove so popular, and spent much of the rest of his life dealing with the popularity that resulted from the poem that bore his name. McGee eventually left the Yukon to build roads in the Lower 48, but returned in the 1930s to find that people were selling urns containing his supposed remains to unsuspecting tourists, a fact that purportedly amused him.

Today, one can still see Sam McGee's real-life cabin in Whitehorse, along with the home where Robert Service wrote his poem that made a road builder one of the most famous 'dead' people in the Yukon. The real Sam McGee lived until 1940, long after the date when he supposedly found himself cremated along the route to the Klondike gold fields.

Travel Bit Number 70: The Overland Trail (Mile 905; Historic Mile 937)

Sometimes called the Old Dawson Trail, the Overland Trail was a wilderness road built from Whitehorse to Dawson City in the early 1900s. Completed in 1902, the White Horse & Yukon Company — the same one that ran the railroad between Skagway and Whitehorse — built the road to deliver mail to the gold fields after taking over the lucrative government mail contract that required regular mail delivery to Dawson City. At 330 miles long, the Overland Trail was approximately seventy miles shorter than the Yukon River route between Whitehorse and Dawson City, and provided a viable alternative route to the River.

Although one could traverse the route in summer, the Overland Trail primarily served winter travelers, when the sternwheelers were unable to make the trek between the Yukon's two primary cities. During the winter, dog sleds traveled the trail and delivered not just mail between the cities, but served as a stagecoach route for passengers, who paid $120 each way — almost $3,475 in today's dollars — for the service. Meals and boarding were not included as part of the price for the five day trip.

From 1902-1914, the Overland Trail provided service three times per week each way in the winter between the two cities, with nearly daily service in the late winter. It remained in regular use for decades after regular service ended, only being entirely replaced with the completion of the highway between Whitehorse and Dawson City in the 1950s. Today, most of the Trail remains in rough or deteriorated form, though a few of the buildings from its heyday as the winter route between Dawson City and Whitehorse. Snowmobilers and dog mushers use the Trail in winter, with bike, ATVs and horses being its primary summer modes of transportation.

Travel Bit Number 71: Takhini Salt Flats (Mile 914)

   As the Alaska Highway leaves Whitehorse on its way to Alaska, small ponds begin to dot the terrain beside the road. Mountains rise above the water in the distance, and if not for their name — the Takhini Salt Flats — no one passing by would likely suspect that these small bodies of water are any different than the hundreds of others that can be seen along other parts of the road. However, as implied by their name, these ponds are salt flats, and much different than those that dot the rest of the landscape along the Alaska Highway.

   The mountains that provide a spectacular backdrop for the Takhini Salt Flats are particularly alkaline (for those who are not scientifically inclined, this means that the mountains are salty). Beneath salt flats is a layer of permafrost, and there is no natural outlet for the water that gathers in the ponds. Salty water flows out of the mountains and into the ponds during spring and summer. Because of the permafrost, though, none of the pond water seeps into the ground below. With no drainage outlet or ability to seep into the aquifer below, the only way for water to escape the ponds is evaporation.

   Thus, the water, with nowhere to go, evaporates and leaves the salt behind, creating the salt flats. Bacteria thrive in these salty waters, creating the white and red edges of the pools that suggest to even a casual observer that these are not normal bodies of water. The saltiness of the ponds is so high that plants normally found only in ocean water — like a red version of sea asparagus — thrive in the Takhini Salt Flats, creating yet another unique feature of the Yukon landscape.

Travel Bit Number 72: A Certain Type of Woman

Although many women came north with their husbands during the gold rush or, in the case of First Nations women, already lived there, the typical woman one thinks of as participating in a gold rush tends to be the woman who has arrived to make money off of her body. During the Klondike gold rush, those women tended to fall into one of two categories: the prostitute or the dance hall girl. The former took the same form it always has; the latter was a woman who performed in a dance hall, either on stage and/or by dancing with men for money. The latter was also supposed to use her feminine wiles to encourage the prospectors to spend their money on dances or the alcohol that flowed in dance halls.

During the Klondike gold rush, there were approximately 200-250 prostitutes in one form or another operating in Dawson City. Some used their jobs as dance hall girls to meet customers, while others operated cigar stores or laundries as legitimate fronts for their prostitution activities. However, most did not hide their profession, and operated freely during the height of the gold rush.

Being a dance hall girl, though, could be a legitimate way for a woman to make money without resorting to prostitution. For $1 or $2 a dance—of which the woman kept half—she would dance with a lonely prospector. She also received half of any liquor sales that could be attributed to her encouragement of the behavior; a dance hall girl could easily earn hundreds of dollars in an evening this way.

While prostitution was technically illegal during the entirety of the gold rush, at the height of the gold rush, the authorities were more concerned with keeping order than dealing with an illegal activity that rarely led to fighting or similar problems. However, in 1901, as the gold rush ended, the authorities began cracking down on prostitution. Once this crackdown occurred, the prostitution went behind closed-doors or moved on to new gold rushes with fewer rules and authorities to enforce the law.

Travel Bit Number 73:

Mendenhall Landing (Mile 927; Historic Mile 960)

At the start of the 20th Century, the White Pass & Yukon Railroad provided an easy mode of transportation into Whitehorse and the interior of the Yukon. From Whitehorse, travelers were more limited in their transportation options. However, thanks to a minor gold rush at Kluane Lake (Travel Bit Number 81), travelers headed in the general direction the Alaska Highway now takes out of Whitehorse had two options. They could either take a rough overland trail or board a sternwheeler to travel about a third of the way to the latest gold fields before meeting up with the trail.

Mendenhall Landing, at the mouth of the Mendenhall River, is where the sternwheelers headed out of Whitehorse were forced to stop their travel. During the minor gold rush at Kluane Lake, this point where the sternwheelers stopped became a meeting point for those who were traveling, lived in the area, or were just looking to see other people in a part of the world where people were still scarce. Large parties were held at Mendenhall Landing at Christmas, and the First Nations communities in the area held baseball games in June. Two or three times a week, the Landing became the sight of dances. When the minor gold rush ended, the sternwheelers continued to provide supplies for those in the vicinity, and until the Alaska Highway was completed, Mendenhall Landing retained its importance as a transfer point for the supplies that made life in this part of the world possible, as well as a social hub for the people who made the area home.

Travel Bit Number 74: Jack London

One of the most famous people drawn to the Klondike gold rush was Jack London, the author and journalist. Jack London arrived in the Yukon after spending only a year at the University of California at Berkeley; his fame and fortune would arise not from his finding of gold in the Yukon, but in later writing about the Yukon and its dogs upon his return to the United States.

Jack London found himself in the Yukon not just to seek fame and fortune, but because of his presumed father. The man, who denied Jack London was his son, wrote the young college student to inform the young man that he was physically unable to have a child. The actual records of Jack London's parentage were destroyed in a fire following the 1906 San Francisco earthquake, so no one has been able to determine if this man was actually named on the birth certificate for Jack London.

Whatever the actual story, the troubling nature of the content of the letter caused the young Jack London to abandon his studies and head to the Yukon. As a prospector, Jack London failed to find the fortune he sought. Even worse, and like many around him, he developed scurvy from a lack of Vitamin C in his diet. He lost his four front teeth during the course of the disease, before heading home.

Back in the United States, Jack London began his writing career, which found its greatest successes in his stories from the time he spent in the Yukon and the gold fields. In 1903, *Call of the Wild* was published. The book told the story of a dog stolen from his California home and taken to Alaska and the Yukon to be sold into the life of a sled dog. *White Fang* appeared in 1906, and told the story of a wild wolf-dog that becomes tame, the reverse of the situation found in *Call of the Wild*.

Travel Bit Number 75: Otter Falls (Mile 965; Historic Mile 995)

Seventeen miles north of where the Alaska Highway now runs sits Otter Falls—a waterfall featured on the 1954 version of Canada's five dollar bill. The waterfall is part of the Aishihik River, formerly known as Canyon Creek. During the spring thaw, huge amounts of water flow over Otter Falls, giving it the majestic look pictured on the old money. However, in the summer, most of the water that would normally flow over the Falls is now diverted to a power turbine, leaving the falls smaller, but still impressive.

The gravel road that leads travelers from the Alaska Highway to Otter Falls continues on to Aishihik Village, approximately 75 miles further up the road. Aishihik Village is now a seasonal hunting and fishing camp for a First Nations community, but it used to be the site of a Northwest Staging Route airbase. Although some of the buildings were built after World War II, many of the buildings date to the original era of the Alaska Highway. These buildings are now slowly returning to nature, having been abandoned together with the airfield in the 1960s.

Travel Bit Number 76: Canyon Creek Bridge (Mile 966; Historic Mile 996)

Every gold rush attracted many people looking to strike it rich quickly and easily, but others came to a gold rush looking to find fortune providing the goods and services that supported the prospectors. With the gold strike at Kluane Lake in 1903, both types arrived in the area. One of the men who arrived was Sam McGee, subject of Robert Service's poem, "The Cremation of Sam McGee." (Travel Bit Number 69.)

Although he did some prospecting, McGee had arrived at the Kluane Lake gold strike with his partner, Gilbert Skelly, to build a road between Whitehorse and Kluane Lake. As part of this project, they erected a simple wooden bridge over a small river then called Canyon Creek. The road would be upgraded over the next forty years, but the bridge continued its service. In 1942, the U.S. Army arrived and dismantled the bridge originally constructed by McGee and Skelly; they rebuilt it in fifteen days.

When the Public Roads Administration followed the U.S. Army, they erected a steel bridge next to the original Alaska Highway bridge; however, they left the wooden bridge intact. Today, after being rebuilt in 1987 and refurbished in 2005, the wooden bridge still stands next to the modern bridge as it crosses Canyon Creek. Although much has changed in the intervening years — including the name of the creek, which is now known as the Aishihik River — the wooden bridge still crosses the Aishihik River as an example of the early bridges that took travelers north to Alaska.

Travel Bit Number 77: Gold Rush Mining Methods

Geologically, the gold found in the Klondike was found in veins. These veins could be forced to the surface—for example, by the force of volcanic or seismic activity—as 'placer gold.' This placer gold is the type of gold one thinks of when thinking about panning for gold; it washes down streams and can be found in loose soil. However, the veins themselves—in which the gold is known as ore—could be found below the surface of creek beds or soil, but there was no predictability as to their location.

Because of the inability to know where gold would ultimately be found, prospectors would first dig a series of 'prospect holes' before commencing full-scale mining. These prospect holes were exactly what they sound like: holes dug into the ground to determine if there was a vein of gold below. If a prospect hole looked promising, the prospector would dig the hole down to the bedrock. The digging process was complicated by the permafrost that covered the region and had to be melted before the soil could be extracted. While there was technology that could quickly and easily get through the permafrost at the time of the Klondike gold rush, the dredges and hydraulic equipment necessary to do so would be impossible to get over the mountain passes that separated the ocean from the gold fields. Thus, miners during the Klondike gold rush resorted to a more laborious method: during the winter, they softened the ground using fires, removed the softened soil into above-ground dump piles, and repeated all winter.

During the summer, the dump piles—which would have remained frozen in place all winter, defying those who might seek to steal the gold within—were passed through sluices. These sluices were a series of wooden boxes about fifteen feet long, through which dirt would be 'washed'—a process where the heavier gold would be separated from the lighter gravel. A single mining operation could need up to twenty sluices to get through the piles of dirt collected during the winter. This process needed huge amounts of water, and thus was only practical during the summer, when the water was not captured in snow or ice.

The use of sluices remained common into the early-1900s in the Klondike and similar gold rushes that followed. However, by the 1910s, dredges began to be used. Dredges create a pool of water below them, before digging up soil and gravel and separating the gold from that gravel in a mostly-automated process.

Today, bulldozers and excavators move soil and gravel to uncover gold-bearing soil. The soil is then passed through a modern version of a sluice to separate the gold. While the modern-day sluice is less crude than those handmade by the miners during the Klondike gold rush, it operates on the same principle and hearkens back to the gold rush era.

Travel Bit Number 78: Haines Junction (Historic Mile 1016; Mile 985)

During the Klondike gold rush, most people starting their journey north by sea crossed the mountains over either the Chilkoot or White Passes near modern-day Skagway, Alaska. However, a third pass over the mountains existed near Haines, Alaska and was used by some people heading to the gold fields: the Chilkat Pass.

For hundreds of years, long before the arrival of the first white people to the area, First Nations groups used the Chilkat Pass. Coastal Tlingit-speaking Chilkats and Southern Tutchone-speaking First Nations groups from the interior would travel between their communities, using the pass over the coastal mountains as a means by which to facilitate both trading and socialization. The Southern-Tutchone speakers called the area near where Haines Junction now sits "Dakwakada," which describes a location where "dakat" — caches of supplies stored high above ground to protect them from animals — stood. Travelers passing along the seasonal routes in the area could use the dakat to sustain themselves on the routes, often heading over the mountains to the coast.

During the gold rush era, the road between Whitehorse and Kluane Lake—now the Alaska Highway—did not pass through Haines Junction, instead passing to the north as it wound toward Kluane Lake. However, the builders of the Alaska Highway routed their road through the town that is now known as Haines Junction, wanting an alternate access route to the ocean that the Chilkat Pass provided. Originally, Haines Junction began as a maintenance camp; its location at the intersection between the Alaska Highway as it continued on to Alaska and the road to Haines and the ocean made the location a natural place for a community. Once Canada took over maintenance of this part of the Alaska Highway after the end of World War II, wives and families of the highway workers based at Haines Junction joined them there, and the maintenance camp became the small town that it is today.

Travel Bit Number 79: The Icefield Ranges (Mile 991)

As the Alaska Highway passes as close as it ever will come to the ocean at Haines Junction and the surrounding area, the mountains guarding the ocean — the Icefield Ranges — become a constant presence to the west of the highway.

The Icefield Ranges consist of two separate groups of mountains. The inland mountains, which are the mountains one sees while driving the Alaska Highway, are the Kluane Range. These mountains average around 8,000 feet in height.

The coastal mountains of the Icefield Ranges, separated from the Kluane Range by a group of narrow valleys and plateaus called the Duke Depression, are the St. Elias Mountains. With many peaks in the 16,000 foot range, the St. Elias Mountains are some of the youngest and tallest mountains in North America. Mount Logan, the tallest mountain in Canada at 19,545 feet, is one of these mountains. Mount St. Elias straddles the border between the United States and Canada, and is the second tallest mountain in both countries at 18,005 feet. In addition to being some of the tallest mountains in North America, the St. Elias Mountains are the highest coastal mountains in the world. Despite their height and proximity to the road, the St. Elias Mountains are generally not visible from the Alaska Highway.

About 3,900 feet up the sides of the mountains of the Icefield Ranges, the spruce fields that cover the bottoms of the mountains give way to treeless slopes. Even in the middle of summer, the tops of the mountains are snow- and ice-covered, giving the mountain ranges their names. These icefields cover the majority of these mountains, and are the largest non-polar icefields in the world.

Travel Bit Number 80: Glaciers

Glaciers have done more to shape the landscape along the Alaska Highway than anything else. Until the first Yukon ice age, the Yukon River flowed into the Pacific Ocean; during that ice age 2.5 million years ago, the giant, glacial ice sheet covering the Yukon blocked the river, creating a giant lake. Eventually, the river reversed its flow, draining northwest through Alaska as it continues to do today. At least six times in the last 2.5 million years, the area along the Alaska Highway has been covered by a glacial ice sheet. During at least one of these ice ages, a land bridge between Alaska and Asia would have been created, allowing animals and humans to cross between the two continents. More recently — about 10,000 years ago — the land that is today Whitehorse was covered by a lake created by a glacier's damming of the Yukon River. The bottom of the lake became covered by glacial silt; one can still see the layer of glacial silt along the course of the Yukon River as it carves its way through the Whitehorse area.

Even today, glaciers continue to shape the landscape. Perhaps most dramatic on this list are the surging glaciers. A surging glacier is a glacier that is moving faster than it normally would for a short period; they can move as fast as 165-300 feet per day. These surging glaciers can quickly dam a river and create lakes that suddenly drain when the glacier recedes, causing major floods. The Yukon has over one hundred currently surging glaciers, some of which are less than thirty miles from the Alaska Highway.

The threat posed by these surging glaciers is quite real; as recently as the 1850s, the area where Haines Junction now sits was covered by a lake formed by the Lowell Glacier's damming of the Alsek River. The Lowell Glacier continues to periodically surge; it last did so in 2009-10. However, a mere 35 miles further down the Alsek River sits the Tweedsmuir Glacier, which surged almost a mile in 2007-08, coming within a few hundred feet of blocking the river. It is likely only a matter of time before a surging glacier creates another lake somewhere near or even on the Alaska Highway.

Travel Bit Number 81: Kluane Lake (Mile 1020)

Although glaciers shaped all of the landscape through which the Alaska Highway travels, Kluane Lake was the site of a glacial event only 300-400 years ago that resulted in major changes to the landscape of the lake. At this time in history, Kluane Lake drained out the south end of the lake. From there, the waters of Kluane Lake flowed approximately 140 miles to the Gulf of Alaska in the Pacific Ocean.

And then, around the time period when European colonization of the east coast of the United States began in earnest, the Kaskawulsh Glacier crossed the river draining out of Kluane Lake. The glacier blocked the sole outlet of the lake at approximately the location where the Slims River sits today, forming a natural dam of the lake's only outlet. Like any dam, water gathered behind the glacier and caused the lake level to rise. In the case of Kluane Lake, this meant the shore of the lake was about thirty feet higher than its present location. More importantly, the lake's drainage reversed. Now, instead of draining to the Pacific Ocean, the lake drained out through the Kluane River on the north end of the lake and into the Yukon River system. With the reversal of the flow of water in and out of Kluane Lake, instead of draining the 140 miles to the Pacific Ocean, the drainage now flowed nearly 15,000 miles to the Bering Sea.

The blocking of the Kluane Lake outlet in the 1700s was the terminal moraine of the Kaskawulsh Glacier — the farthest the Glacier ever reached in its slow movement. Today, the Kaskawulsh Glacier has retreated far into the Icefield Ranges above Kluane Lake, though it is still over 215 miles long and covers over 15,500 square miles. Although the Kaskawulsh Glacier has now retreated and the water level has lowered, the reversal of the flow of water in Kluane Lake remained permanent.

Today, you can still see the high water mark during the era of the glacier, many feet above the Alaska Highway. These high water marks are quickly recognized because there are what appear to be beaches that sit high on the hills surrounding the Lake, far from the water that once lapped at their sandy shores.

Travel Bit Number 82: Silver City (Mile 1021)

In 1903, Dawson Charlie — one of the original discoverers of the Klondike gold (Travel Bit Number 59) — staked the first claim of the minor Kluane gold rush, which took place in the streams around Kluane Lake. By the end of 1903, over 2,000 claims had been made as part of this minor gold rush. These minor gold rushes were not uncommon during this era; similar events took place in Nome, Alaska and Atlin, British Columbia.

Like Dawson City before it, Silver City became the central city of the gold rush. Where Dawson City had been the end of the sternwheeler line from Whitehorse, Silver City found itself at the end of the Kluane Wagon Road, which began in Whitehorse.

Unfortunately for those who staked claims as part of the Kluane gold rush, it was not the hoped-for major strike. By the 1920s, the claims had been abandoned. Silver City, briefly a bustling gold rush town, was abandoned as well. Today, its buildings sit near Kluane Lake, falling down and being slowly reclaimed by nature. The biggest legacy from that time period was the Kluane Wagon Road which had taken the original prospectors to Kluane Lake, and which the U.S. Army mostly followed when building the Alaska Highway.

Travel Bit Number 83: Soldier's Summit (Mile 1030; Historic Mile 1061)

In November 1942, on a previously unremarkable hillside overlooking Kluane Lake, the U.S. Army held the small ceremony commemorating the completion of the Alaska Highway. Today, in honor of the event, the hillside where the ceremony took place is known as Soldiers' Summit, and a small hike takes visitors to the location where the official opening ceremony for the highway took place.

At the time of the opening ceremony for the Alaska Highway — still known as ALCAN at that time — the highway ran right next to the ceremony site, affording a breathtaking view for travelers. Besides Kluane Lake, the site looked toward the Icefield Ranges; at the time of the ceremony, many of the peaks of the St. Elias Mountains remained to be explored and even named, despite being some of the tallest mountains in North America.

In the days leading up to the opening ceremony, a warm front moved into the southern part of the Alaska Highway. The formerly frozen rivers the new road crossed began to thaw, and the resulting floes destroyed several bridges. Thus, the opening ceremony for the Alaska Highway took place on a day when the highway itself was not actually open from beginning to end. In fairness, though, only one bridge remained out at the time of the ceremony and it would be repaired the next day.

Although the days leading up to the ceremony opening the Alaska Highway had been unseasonably warm for November in northern Canada, the day of the opening ceremony was anything but warm—it dawned with snow squalls and a temperature of -15° Fahrenheit. By the time of the opening ceremony around 9:30 AM, things had not improved weather-wise. The band providing music for the ceremony had to wait inside heated tents because their instruments would freeze almost immediately if they stepped outside. Even more telling about the temperature, a group of Mounties attending the ceremony only made it halfway through before they ran for the heated tents to change from their tunics and boots into fur caps, buffalo coats and winter boots.

Despite the cold weather, the ceremony went off with as much spectacle as a war time ceremony of its sort in the middle of a virtually uninhabited part of the world could muster. More important than the ceremony, though, was that the Alaska Highway was open for travel. During the month of November 1942, over 1,000 trucks would drive some portion of the highway. Although the road that existed at the time of the opening ceremony is not the major highway that now exists, it was the start of what would become the highway that now provides a vital mode of transportation across a large portion of Canada and into Alaska.

Travel Bit Number 84: Caribou

One of the animals travelers on the Alaska Highway are sometimes lucky enough to see are caribou. The only member of the deer family where both males and females have antlers, the females actually keep their antlers longer than their male counterparts. Before losing their antlers, females use them to claim and protect feeding areas for their calves before losing them. Evidence of caribou in the Yukon dates back to around 1.6 million years ago.

Today, there are two main types of caribou one can see along the Alaska Highway or areas near the Alaska Highway: woodland caribou and migratory/barren-ground caribou. Woodland caribou are typically found in small herds, and they move between the forest and tundra depending on the time of year. Migratory caribou are typically found in giant herds and undertake a long, annual migration. These migratory caribou are the sort one typically thinks of when thinking of caribou, though the former are the ones travelers on the Alaska Highway are most likely to see.

There are several groups of woodland caribou who make the area around Kluane Lake home. These caribou are typically on the high mountains around the lake, and can be seen climbing among their peaks. There are dozens of herds of woodland caribou across the Yukon, though the herds at Kluane Lake are some of the easier to see along its length.

The migratory caribou, unlike the woodland caribou, travel across the Yukon and Alaska. The major herd of these migratory caribou in this part of the world is the Porcupine herd, which is named after its birthing grounds along the Porcupine River in Alaska. At approximately 197,000 animals and growing, the Porcupine herd ranges across Alaska, the Yukon and the Northwest Territory, and can venture as far south as the Alaska Highway. Their territory covers 155,000 square miles — an area the size of Wyoming. During the summer, the Porcupine herd gathers in groups of 10,000 animals or more while traveling to the coast and ice fields in search of relief from the relentless mosquitoes that plague them during the summer. One summer, the herd that gathered for relief from the mosquitoes was estimated at 93,000 animals.

Travel Bit Number 85: Destruction Bay (Mile 1051; Historic Mile 1083)

After the completion of the Alaska Highway, driving the road during World War II was still a difficult and dangerous proposition. Getting from Dawson Creek to Delta Junction was not the comparatively easy trip along a paved highway that it is today.

Destruction Bay sits on the south shore of Kluane Lake, one of a few small communities along the lakeshore. Unlike the other communities, however, Destruction Bay does not trace its history to the Kluane gold rush.

Destruction Bay came into being during World War II as a relay station along the Alaska Highway. Placed at 100 mile intervals, these relay stations served as a place for drivers to get a rest and meal when traveling the road. Each of the relay stations had garages to get trucks and vehicles serviced—a definite requirement on a road where certain stretches were still "paved" with logs and wooden planks. There were bunks for sleeping, places to eat, and the very necessary gas pumps.

While Destruction Bay came into being as a relay station, its beginning as that relay station was ignominious. Before construction on the station was completed, a Kluane Lake storm — known for their ferocity and hurricane-force wind — destroyed the still unfinished station. The relay station got its name, and the second version of the relay station was built without further incident. Now, the relay station is gone, but the community that grew up around it remains and retains the name.

Travel Bit Number 86: Burwash Landing / Lu'an Man (Mile 1061; Historic Mile 1093)

In the early 1900s, Eugene and Louis Jacquot arrived on the shores of Kluane Lake. The brothers—who were trained French chefs who had originally arrived in the Yukon seeking their fortunes with the Klondike gold rush—were probably not the sort of people most would expect to find in the Yukon, but the lure of gold affected men of all sorts. Having failed to strike it rich in the Klondike, the brothers built a trading post on the shores of Kluane Lake during the Kluane Lake gold rush, where they made their fortune over the next decades.

After opening their successful trading post, the Jacquot brothers branched out by starting a guiding service. The service was started with Tom Dickson, a member of the Northwest Mounted Police whom the brothers had met on their way to the Klondike years earlier. The guiding service proved lucrative; rich individuals would pay thousands of dollars to go on sixty day, guided pack trips. Individuals on the trips would arrive in Whitehorse, then go by wagon to Kluane Lake. From there, they would head into the wilderness by horse, enjoying unspoiled lands and fine French food along the way.

The Jacquot brothers were still in Burwash Landing running their trading post and guide service when the U.S. Army arrived to build the Alaska Highway. Their trading post quickly became known as the best place to eat along the entirety of the long road; they had fresh produce and even a herd of cows when the Americans arrived—and French chefs to make the meals. By 1945, the Jacquot brothers had built a lodge to serve travelers on the Alaska Highway. While the brothers passed away shortly after the opening of the road, their descendants operated it for many years before closing.

Today, Burwash Landing is the administrative center for the Kluane First Nation community. Visitors to the small town on the shores of Kluane Lake are treated to signs in the Southern Tutchone language; the Southern Tutchone Athabascans were the first people to live in what is now Burwash Landing, when they used the location as a seasonal camp.

Travel Bit Number 87: A Long Range Language

      The first inhabitants of the Yukon arrived 20,000 to 45,000 years ago, though not much is known about those early people. This fact should be somewhat obvious from the inability to narrow the time of their arrival in the Yukon to a period consisting of fewer than 25,000 years. In all likelihood, these first individuals to arrive in the Yukon were the ancestors of today's First Nations men and women.

      Sometime around 720 A.D., Mount Churchill, a volcano in the St. Elias Mountains along the Canada-Alaska border, erupted and covered much of the Yukon with a layer of ash up to two feet thick as part of one of the largest North American eruptions in the last two thousand years. You can still see this layer of ash when the Alaska Highway is cut through the earth; it is located just below the initial layer of soil. Although there is no written record from this time period for the First Nations men and women who continue to live in this part of the world, they have passed down stories from this moment in time, when all the animals and fish died as a result of the eruption.

Oddly enough, a group of Native Americans in the southwestern part of the United States have passed down remarkably similar stories from this same moment in time, despite being over 3,000 miles away. On its own, this fact is just an interesting coincidence. However, both of these communities speak remarkably similar languages, which have descended from the same rare language. The group of southwestern Native Americans who speak this language are isolated in terms of language. Not only are they the only community in the southwest to speak this rare language, but the nearest community who speaks a similar language resides in the Pacific Northwest and is connected to the First Nations people in the Yukon. Indeed, during World War II when Navajo men from the American southwest arrived in Alaska to train as code talkers for the U.S. Army, they were immediately able to talk with these members of the First Nations in their own language.

With these coincidences in mind, some theorize that the eruption of Mount Churchill led to the migration of some of the ancestors of today's First Nations inhabitants of the Yukon to the southwest in a search for food. While this has been neither confirmed nor validated, it seems a likely basis for the odd distribution of the language spoken by these Native Americans and First Nations communities.

Travel Bit Number 88: Permafrost (Mile 1104)

The most difficult portion of the Alaska Highway to build was not a pass over a mountain or a road carved out of rock, but instead the relatively flat stretch and seemingly uncomplicated stretch of road between Kluane Lake and the Alaska-Canada border. The reason is not something one can see, but the ground itself. Instead of regular soil, the ground in this area is one of the most difficult types of soil in the world on which to build anything: permafrost.

Permafrost is soil that has been at or below the freezing point for two or more years. Sometimes, it is rock or sediment instead of soil. On top of the permafrost, there is a layer of soil, rock or sediment that freezes and thaws annually, which his called the active layer. However, the actual permafrost below, as its name implies, is more or less permanently frozen.

There is little that would indicate that the soil in this part of the world is any different than regular soil. It grows plants and trees, and on its surface, there is nothing to indicate the differences below ground. Were one to walk on it during the summer, it would feel like other soil. The only easily noticeable feature of the permafrost in this area is the "drunken forest" effect — with short root systems and shifting soils beneath them, the trees grow haphazardly, and are shorter than normal.

The most easily noticed effects of the permafrost are found on the road itself. Not only was the road above the permafrost the most difficult section to build, it remains the most difficult section of the Alaska Highway to maintain. When a road is constructed over permafrost, like the portion between Kluane Lake and the Alaska-Canada border, the permafrost below melts, and the ground level rises and sinks with this melting process — taking the road with it as it does.

While there is still no good solution for building a road over permafrost, there have been many attempts to do so since the construction of the Alaska Highway. However, despite the regular maintenance required to keep up a road built over permafrost, including regular reconstruction of such roads and experiments in road building, the section of the road past Burwash Landing was, for many years, the original road built by the U.S. Army. This original road was not what one thinks of as a road, but was a corduroy road — a road that consisted of logs buried in the permafrost or boggy lands along the route of the road, which were then covered with gravel to create a very crude and bumpy road. The Alaska Highway remained in this state for decades.

Sometime in the 1980s, the government "paved" the Alaska Highway out of Burwash Landing by chip sealing the gravel of the corduroy road, but it only proved to be a temporary fix to a problem that had plagued the road since its initial building. In the 1990s, the government finally replaced the road, which required an entire rebuilding and rerouting of approximately seventy miles of the Alaska Highway. Despite the needed work to rebuild the road, the nature of the area means that even a brand new road will not last long, until a better method to deal with permafrost as a road base is discovered.

Travel Bit Number 89: Beringea

Although the area along the Alaska Highway has been shaped by glacial activity over the course of the last several million years, the lack of glacial activity has also proven to be a major force for changing the landscape, and the best example of this is Beringia.

During much of the ice ages, a large area stretching from Siberia to Alaska and the Yukon remained ice free. During this era, a major portion of the Bering Strait would have been dry land, with much of the world's water caught up in the ice sheets that covered huge expanses of the continents. These ice sheets and the Arctic Ocean surrounded Beringea, creating an isolated grassland steppe that stretched thousands of miles across what is today a large portion of the Arctic, Alaska, the Yukon and Siberia.

A few thousand people survived in Beringea, isolated from other human populations for at least 5,000 years. Beringea also served as a unique ecosystem in a largely glaciated area, where animals such as mammoths, mastadons and relatives of the sabre-toothed tiger roamed. Plants that today only thrive much further south grew on the grassland at various times during this period as well, as it would sometimes experience warmer periods.

Eventually, the ice sheet that covered North America retreated, and the ocean levels rose. Those humans who had lived in Beringea traveled south and populated North and South America and Siberia was once again cut off from North America. The lack of a glacier allowed humans to survive and eventually populate the Americas, just as other glaciers created the landscape through which those same humans migrated.

Travel Bit Number 90: Snag (Mile 1153)

The village of Snag looks like your typical community along the Alaska Highway, but it is anything but typical. Formerly the site of an airport on the Northwest Staging Route, Snag is now a tiny village with fewer residents than some families have children. However, Snag has one defining moment in its history: it recorded the coldest temperature ever in North America.

Only a month into 1947, and Snag had already recorded two record-setting cold days. Meteorologists at the Northwest Staging Route airport were cut off from the rest of the world; it was so cold that supply flights could not land.

On February 3, 1947, it was particularly cold. The thermometers had bottomed out at   -80° Fahrenheit; the mercury had dropped into the bulb and couldn't go any lower, even as the temperature did exactly that. The airport itself was about three miles outside of the village of Snag, but when the meteorologists had to venture outside, they could hear the village dogs barking, thanks to the dense air and cold that had settled in. The dog's harnesses were made out of leather; if they moved, the harnesses immediately cracked and broke. Some types of metal snapped if bent and wood had turned into rock-like logs.

Although the meteorologists and others living at the airport did not spend much time outside, when they did, they couldn't breathe deeply, or they risked getting freezer burn on their lungs. When they exhaled, their breath froze instantly, and fell to the ground as white powder. It tinkled as it hit the ground, like bits of glass hitting the snow.

Ultimately, the temperature reached -81.4° Fahrenheit, a North American record that still stands sixty years later.

Travel Bit Number 91: Beaver Creek (Mile 1167; Historic Mile 1202)

Beaver Creek is the last town along the Canadian portion of the Alaska Highway for travelers headed north to Alaska. It is also the westernmost city in Canada. Not only is it a full 18° of longitude west of Vancouver, it is so far west that it shares a meridian line with some islands of the South Pacific. At a mere sixteen miles from Snag, home of the coldest winter temperature ever recorded in North America (Travel Bit Number 90), and with an average yearly high of 34.5° Fahrenheit and an average January high of -4.7° Fahrenheit, it should go without saying that the South Pacific has a far different climate than that of Beaver Creek, even though they share a meridian line.

During the building of the Alaska Highway, Beaver Creek became the location of arguably the most important moment in the history of the road. While Contact Creek (Travel Bit Number 46) marked the point where the southern half of the road was completed, Beaver Creek was where the Alaska Highway was the place where the last bit of highway came together to complete the road to Alaska. Just outside the modern town of Beaver Creek, a bulldozer working from the north ran into a bulldozer working from the south to connect the last two unfinished stretches of the Alaska Highway, thus completing the road.

As the two bulldozers met, a photographer arrived to take a picture of the historic moment. The resulting picture of the meeting and completion of the Alaska Highway went out across the United States: a black man from Philadelphia, Refines Sims, Jr., stood to the left on the picture, shaking hands with Alfred Jalufka, a white man from Texas, on the right. Sims smiles broadly, while Jalufka adopts a more serious face, a cigarette dangling from his lip. In an era when not just the Army but much of the country remained segregated, this picture showed the reality of life along the Alaska Highway, where black and white soldiers worked at the same jobs in different battalions. While the soldiers and their work was segregated, they were all invaluable to the completion of the Alaska Highway.

Travel Bit Number 92: America in Canada

The oldest town in the Yukon is Forty Mile. Established as a mining town in the late 1880s, Forty Mile is approximately twenty miles on the Yukon side of the Alaska-Canada border. During the search for gold near Forty Mile, the Americans who showed up in search of gold decided to claim the area around Forty Mile for the United States. They not only gave the town a name (Mitchell, Alaska), they even opened up a post office, because, as everyone knows, if you can get your bills somewhere, it is definitely a real place. The Mounties learned of this and came in to kick out the Americans. Any Americans who wanted to stay and work their claims in the gold fields were required to admit the town was actually in Canada.

The problems of Americans mining in Canada were not limited to territorial disputes. Many Americans set out for the Klondike gold rush thinking they were headed to a place in Alaska, not Canada; there were maps showing exactly this situation. The problem was exacerbated by the path most Americans took to the gold fields; they headed through Skagway, in Alaska's panhandle, to start their lives in the Yukon. Thus, they landed in Alaska, and only crossed into Canada somewhere along their journey to the gold fields.

Once arriving in Dawson City and the Klondike gold fields, prospectors found themselves less than thirty miles from the Alaska border; Eagle City was a mere eight miles from the site of the main gold strike on the Alaska side of the U.S.-Canada border. As many as eighty percent of those prospecting were American; thus, the city had a large and perhaps majority American population. Canadian authorities limited the size of mining claims afforded to Americans and levied a ten percent tax on gold, which didn't please many Americans. Finding this situation unbearable, some Americans immediately left the Klondike and set out for gold fields in Alaska; others smuggled their gold into Alaska after mining it in Canada to avoid the tax they viewed as unfair.

Travel Bit Number 93: Canada-U.S. Border (Mile 1186; Historic Mile 1221)

At Historic Mile 1221 of the Alaska Highway, the road crosses the border between Canada and the United States. There are no customs and immigration checkpoints directly on the border; the Canadian checkpoint is approximately 20 miles away in Beaver Creek, while the American checkpoint is about a quarter mile further north on the Alaska Highway. The actual border is marked by a parking lot and several signs and markers where travelers can stop for pictures as they straddle a small portion of the longest unprotected international border in the world.

Standing on the Canada-U.S. border on the Alaska Highway, a historical artifact is readily apparent. Along the border itself, a twenty food wide swath has been cut. As far as the border stretches across the landscape, one can follow the swath through the wilderness. This cut through the forest dates to 1918, when crews initially cut the border so that people would know they were on the border between the two countries. It's not just a cut along the border between Canada and Alaska; one can see the same cut as far away as the border in Maine and Vermont, as it extends the entire portion of the forested border (about 1,350 miles of the 5,525 mile border between the two countries is forested).

This cut through the woods—known in some places as "The Slash"—extends ten feet on either side of the border. Approximately every fifteen to twenty-five years, crews clear the cut; it takes about five or six summers to complete the job in Alaska. Some parts of the border require more frequent trimming than others; in Southeastern Alaska where the temperate and rainy climate allows for faster growth, there is a need for more frequent upkeep on the border.

Although it appears there is nothing in the cleared area, there are 191 border monuments stretching along its length between Canada and Alaska. One monument is placed every three to four miles, where it can be sighted with surveying equipment from the previous monument. These monuments form the official border of the two countries, though they do sometimes disappear or get destroyed. Monument Number One on the border is located on the Beaufort Sea. Not only has it been washed away twice over the last century, but its original site no longer exists, it too having been washed away by erosion.

Travel Bit Number 94: Seward's Folly

On March 30, 1867, Secretary of State William H. Seward reached an agreement with Russia to sell the United States the huge portion of North America now known as Alaska. At the time, many decried Seward's purchase as "Seward's Folly," suspecting the United States had just spent $7.2 million for a place covered in ice, with no redeeming qualities. This opinion was reflected in other nicknames given to the newly purchased land, such as "Polar Bear Garden," "Icebergia," and "Walrussia."

On April 9, 1867, the Senate ratified the treaty providing for the purchase of Alaska by a margin of one vote. For about two cents an acre, the United States officially purchased Alaska, deadly animals and oil deposits included.

While many criticized the purchase at the time, the move ultimately proved extremely valuable. Immediately, the purchase lessened Britain and Russia as rivals to the United States in the Pacific region, and helped cement a good relationship between Russia and the United States. By the time gold was discovered in the region by the end of the 19th Century, any remaining opposition to the treaty had disappeared.

Travel Bit Number 95: Chisana Gold Rush (Mile 1234; Historic Mile 1271)

In 1913, the last of the gold rushes of the gold rush era began in Chisana City, Alaska. While there would be a few small gold strikes after 1913, none would be the sort of heavily-publicized strike that attracted thousands to a far-flung location to seek their fame and fortune. Two major factors brought the era to a close. First, the advent of modern mining and mining techniques had begun to make prospecting obsolete. Second, with the start of World War I, many of those who would otherwise have found themselves in gold fields found themselves fighting a war or otherwise unable to participate in a gold rush.

Like other gold strikes of the era, the Chisana gold rush attracted thousands to its location high in the Wrangell Mountains. For just a few, fleeting years, men and women trekked to Chisana City looking for gold and their fortunes; by the 1920s, Chisana City had been abandoned. It was the typical tale of a gold rush city, though at the time, no one knew it would be the last of its kind.

Chisana City is not along the Alaska Highway, but instead sits high in the Wrangell Mountains. However, one can see the Chisana City area from the road, and those seeking an adventure can trek to the site, either by foot or horseback. Those who are seeking less of an adventure and have money to spare can fly to the area. While about two dozen people now live in the area seasonally, mining the creeks in much the same way as those who participated in the gold rush did, many more come to the area every summer to see the still-standing ghost town of Chisana City. Because of its inaccessibility, Chisana City, and its companion city of Bonanza City are preserved exactly as they were in the gold rush era — they were abandoned as they stood, right down to the home furnishings. There are still two ghost towns, tent camps, water diversion systems for mining, the remnants of transportation systems built for the miners and, of course, mining equipment. While other gold rush towns recreate the era, Chisana City remains just as it stood when it became the last gold strike of the era.

Travel Bit Number 96: Tetlin Junction (Mile 1267; Historic Mile 1306)

The first time the Alaska Highway crosses another major road once it reaches Alaska is at Tetlin Junction, where the Taylor Highway branches north from the Alaska Highway as it heads toward Chicken, Alaska and back to Canada and Dawson City via the Top of the World Highway. The Top of the World Highway got its name from its location, which is almost entirely above the tree line. The road is only open during the summer, and on the Canadian side, it remains mostly gravel. By the end of September, with the first heavy snows of the year, the Taylor Highway and Top of the World Highway close, cutting off the few small communities along their lengths from vehicular traffic.

Although today there is little to note at Tetlin Junction, for years, it was home to one of the original private businesses built solely to service tourists and travelers on the newly-built Alaska Highway. This business — the Forty Mile Roadhouse — was opened in 1949. Its owners had leased the land for the Roadhouse in 1948, the year the Alaska Highway officially opened. Until approximately 1985, the business operated in some form; today, the buildings are gone, but one can still see some of their remnants along the road.

On August 16, 2013, Tetlin Junction was the site of an incredible natural phenomenon: a fire tornado, also known as a firenado. Although the forest fire near Tetlin Junction was one of the smaller fires in Alaska that year, one would not have known it from the firenado that accompanied it. The firenado measured three-quarters of a mile wide and soared thousands of feet into the sky. A firefighter filming the fire from a helicopter happened to capture the event on film; otherwise, with its remote location, no one would have known the event occurred.

Travel Bit Number 97: Sand Dunes of Alaska (Mile 1267; Historic Mile 1306)

As described in Travel Bit Number 96, Tetlin Junction is the location where the Taylor Highway branches off of the Alaska Highway as it heads north and into Canada. As one crosses the actual junction of the two roads, the land to the side of the road is sandy. However, this isn't just sand left from winter travelers looking to grain traction or builders of the road. As it turns out, the hills that surround Tetlin Junction are not actually hills, but sand dunes.

Over 10,000 years ago, fine particles of sand from the Tanana River—a river that the Alaska Highway crosses shortly after leaving Tetlin Junction—blew from the river bed toward the nearby mountains at Tetlin Junction. Over time, the sand dunes built up, until they formed the landscape that travelers now see. In between the dunes, one can see small depressions; these often fill with water and create small ponds and lakes.

The sand from the dunes is mostly gray; it has also been there long enough to gain a layer of soil and other sediment on top of it. Thus, while the hills in this area are sand dunes, they are not the sort of sand dunes that one sees at the beach.

Other locations in Alaska and the Yukon have more typical large sand dunes. In the Yukon, just a short trip off of the Alaska Highway, lies the Carcross Desert. The Carcross Desert is not a true desert, but a large group of sand dunes that formed when glacial lakes deposited their sand, before drying up and leaving just the sandy bottom of the former lakes behind.

North of the Arctic Circle lies Kobuk Valley National Park, one of the least visited National Parks in the U.S. The sand dunes at Kobuk Valley were created by the deposits left by retreating glaciers and strong winds. As with the sand dunes at Tetlin Junction, those at Kobuk Valley are covered by sediment, forests and, because of its location, tundra. The sand and harsh conditions at Kobuk Valley are so extreme that NASA uses the Park as a stand-in for the polar dunes of Mars.

Travel Bit Number 98: Tok
(Mile 1279; Historic Mile 1314)

No one knows how the city of Tok—rhymes with 'soak' or 'choke'—got its name.

One theory is that Tok is a Native word. Supposedly, the Native American community in the area referred to a nearby river as the Tok or Tokai River as late as the early 1900s, and the city that grew up nearby took on the name of the river that still flows near town.

Others believe that the name Tok is a shortened form of the word "Tokyo." The present-day site of the city was established during World War II, when Tokyo—and the very real possibility that the soldiers working on the Alaska Highway might get an unplanned and undesired trip to that city in their near future—was in the forefront of the minds of Americans.

Still other suggest that the name also belonged to the mascot of a group of engineers working on the Alaska Highway; the name of the town per this story thus came from a beloved dog.

There are also more than a few visitors to Tok who claim the name came from a certain activity involved with the cannabis plant, though one suspects that those who prefer this theory may have been partaking a little too much in said activity.

No matter how it got its name, when it was built during World War II, Tok was sometimes referred to as "Million Dollar Camp." The nickname was a nod to the amount that had been spent to build and maintain the small city as a roadside town and camp. Today, the Chamber of Commerce has dubbed the city "The Coldest Inhabited Community in North America," which likely attracts an entirely different sort of person than its actual name does.

Travel Bit Number 99: Northern Lights

While most of those who drive the Alaska Highway do so during the summer, those who travel the road during the winter months are almost guaranteed to be treated to the sight of the *aurora borealis* — the northern lights. From late August to April, the northern lights put on a show that is almost unparalleled anywhere else in the world. Travelers from around the world arrive in the Canadian and Alaskan wilderness to see the dancing lights, often partaking of tours that exist solely to look at them. There is a belief supposedly held by some from Japan that conceiving a baby under the northern lights is auspicious, and a baby thus conceived will prove to be a gifted child. While this is an unverified claim, it is oft-repeated and persists despite its unverifiable nature.

The northern lights are caused by collisions between gaseous particles in the earth's atmosphere and charged particles released by the sun entering the earth's atmosphere. The colors of the northern lights, which can range across the color spectrum but are usually green or pink, are caused by the type of particles involved in the collisions. The lights themselves usually appear as dancing lights, but can also appear as patches of lights, arcs, shooting rays and dancing curtains. The lights extend anywhere from fifty to four hundred miles above the surface of the earth, creating a beautiful sight that can sometimes be seen as far south as New Orleans, given the correct conditions. However, the area along the Alaska Highway from Whitehorse to its end is noted for the particularly fine show it gets from the northern lights.

Travel Bit Number 100: Opening the Alaska Highway to Travelers

After World War II ended, the Alaska Highway remained closed to civilian traffic. However, in 1948, the road officially opened for its first tourist season. The road as traveled by those first intrepid tourists was not the paved highway that greets today's travelers. Instead, of the 1,420 miles that opened to the public in 1948, 970 miles still consisted of the original pioneer road built by the U.S. Army in 1942. Although it had been substantially improved from the dirt path through the woods that had been the first highway, this was still little more than a gravel road through the wilderness.

As a wilderness road, that first year, things did not go well for tourists who arrived in cars ill-equipped to handle a pioneer road. The road claimed so many vehicles during the first summer weeks that the authorities quickly closed the road to tourists before the season ended. However, a year later, the authorities reopened the Alaska Highway to year-round tourist traffic, and ever since, it has been a magnet for travelers looking for an adventure and epic road trip.

Travel Bit Number 101: Delta Junction (Mile 1387; Historic Mile 1422)

The Alaska Highway comes to an end at Delta Junction, where it meets the Richardson Highway. Just as at the beginning of the road almost 1,400 miles earlier, Delta Junction provides visitors with an opportunity to take a picture with monuments dedicated to its end of the Alaska Highway. From Delta Junction, visitors can head south toward Anchorage or continue north to Fairbanks.

Or, for those who haven't had enough of one of North America's great drives, one can turn around and drive the Alaska Highway all over again.

Additional Books in the Travel Bits Series

The Overseas Highway

Coming Soon

Gettysburg
Key West
Las Vegas
The Oregon Trail
Pacific Coast Highway
Yellowstone National Park

Made in the USA
San Bernardino, CA
18 November 2017